# THE
# PREDICTABLE
# FAILURE
# OF
# EDUCATIONAL
# REFORM

*Seymour B. Sarason*

# THE PREDICTABLE FAILURE OF EDUCATIONAL REFORM

## Can We Change Course Before It's Too Late?

Jossey-Bass Publishers
San Francisco • Oxford • 1990

THE PREDICTABLE FAILURE OF EDUCATIONAL REFORM
*Can We Change Course Before It's Too Late?*
by Seymour B. Sarason

Copyright © 1990 by: Jossey-Bass Inc., Publishers
350 Sansome Street
San Francisco, California 94104
&
Jossey-Bass Limited
Headington Hill Hall
Oxford OX3 0BW

**Library of Congress Cataloging-in-Publication Data**

Sarason, Seymour Bernard, date.
    The predictable failure of educational reform : can we change
course before it's too late? / Seymour B. Sarason.
    p.    cm. — (The Jossey-Bass education series) (The Jossey-
Bass social and behavioral science series)
    Includes bibliographical references and index.
    ISBN 1-55542-269-1
    1. Educational change—United States.  2. Education—United
States—Evaluation.  3. Educational planning—United States.
I. Title.  II. Series.  III. Series: The Jossey-Bass social and
behavioral science series.
LA217.S27   1990
370'.973—dc20                                          90-40656
                                                           CIP

Manufactured in the United States of America

The paper in this book meets the guidelines for
permanence and durability of the Committee on
Production Guidelines for Book Longevity of the
Council on Library Resources.


JACKET DESIGN BY WILLI BAUM



FIRST EDITION

*Code 9080*

A joint publication in
The Jossey-Bass Education Series and
The Jossey-Bass Social and Behavioral Science Series

*To those who made April 22–23, 1989, in
New Haven such a memorable experience.
Thanks.*

# Contents

# Preface

THIS BOOK IS NOT LIKELY TO WIN ME FRIENDS. INDEED, I MAY
lose some. I wrote it to discharge the obligation to myself to
state frankly and succinctly conclusions to which I reluctantly
have come. If that reluctance, better yet resistance, was strong,
it was because I did not want to confront the past inadequacies
in my own thinking. No less than most people, I was caught
up in a way of thinking about schools that essentially assumed
that certain axioms on which reform efforts were based were
valid. Once you flush out these axioms you are hoist by your
own petard because you now see the educational scene differently, and it makes quite a difference. If it took me years to
arrive at this point, I do not expect others to respond enthusiastically. The problem is not what to do but how to think,
how to take seriously the idea that there is a universe of alternative explanations for past failures of reform. Some wit—I
think it was Mencken—said that for any problem there is a
simple, direct answer that is wrong. That kind of answer has
not been in short supply in the arena of educational problems,
and I am not exempting myself from that criticism. Fortunately, and for reasons about which I am not all that clear, I

have had little trouble accepting my imperfections and limitations as a thinker. Problems are constants; answers are provisional.

What I say in this book has been said by others, past and present. If anything is distinctive about what I say, it inheres in two features: emphasis and interrelating ideas heretofore kept separate. My hope is that the reader will come to view educational reform from a new perspective. If on the level of action this perspective is troublesome because it does not provide simple answers, it is in part because it is an unfamiliar perspective. If familiarity breeds contempt, unfamiliarity breeds rejection. No one warmly seeks, let alone embraces, significant intellectual and personal change.

This book is intended for two audiences, one relatively homogeneous and the other very heterogeneous. The first audience is what is conventionally termed the community of educators: teachers, administrators, the faculties of our colleges of education, and researchers in the social sciences who have studied schools. That is the audience I have primarily addressed in my previous publications. The second audience consists of legislators and policymakers who are not in a formal sense educators but whose role and power mightily affect the direction of educational reform. It also includes foundations for whom educational research and reform are explicit obligations, as well as that increasing number of business leaders who seek to influence the effort to improve our schools. Needless to say, it also includes that much larger number of individuals (for example, parents) who are both anxious about and puzzled by the lack of improvement from past efforts.

In trying to reach such a wide audience, I in no way sought to water down the substance and complexity of the issues I consider crucial. Frankly, as I see them, the issues are not all that complex. Complexity is not an issue; ignoring the obvious is, and it is the obvious that this book seeks to bring to people's attention.

In brief, Chapter One discusses the inability of reformers to confront the intractability of schools to past efforts at change and why that omission dooms present efforts. Chapter Two takes up the different obstacles that those within and without the school culture encounter in realistically comprehending the dynamics of school systems, and it examines why it is erroneous to view these systems as unique. Chapter Three concerns the nature of power relationships in schools and shows why the failure of reformers to address issues of power ensures that desired changes will not be achieved. Chapter Four takes up the issues surrounding the question of who should be involved in educational decision making. A comparison is made between those issues in the educational arena and in the private sector, with emphasis on the work of Carl Frost with the Scanlon Plan in the private sector. Chapter Five asserts that unless altering power relationships among different levels of educational personnel is concomitant with altering power relationships in the classroom, the goals of reform will not be realized. The significance of the research on cooperative learning is discussed. Chapter Six presents five examples to illustrate why efforts at educational change are rarely successful. Three of the examples concern medical education, emphasizing how in those settings intractability is no less a feature than in public schools. Chapter Seven takes up the differences between the imitation and replication of presumably successful change efforts and describes why true replication is so rare. Special emphasis is given to efforts that have received much attention in the mass media but for which there is no evidence that efforts at duplication were truly replications or successful. Chapter Eight argues that the unreflective acceptance of the belief that schools exist only or primarily for children is one of the root causes of intractability. Schools should exist equally for the development of both faculty and students. Finally, Chapter Nine asks and discusses these questions: What are or should be our goals for students? Why are schools uninteresting places? Despite the emotional rhetoric, why do we continue to teach subject matter, not students? Why are the interests and curiosities of children not related to what children experience in the classroom?

Schools have been intractable to change and the attainment of goals set by reformers. A major failure has been the inability of reformers to confront this intractability. As a result, each new wave of reform learns nothing from earlier efforts and comes up with recommendations that have failed in the past. What is called reform is based on an acceptance of the system as it has been and is. Change will not occur unless there is an alteration of power relationships among those in the system and within the classroom. Altering these power relationships is necessary, but it is not a sufficient condition for obtaining desired changes. This is especially true for proposals that seek to give a greater role in decision making to teachers. There are two basic issues. The first is the assumption that schools exist primarily for the growth and development of children. That assumption is invalid because teachers cannot create and sustain the conditions for the productive development of children if those conditions do not exist for teachers. The second issue is that there is now an almost unbridgeable gulf that students perceive between the world of the school and the world outside of it. Schools are uninteresting places in which the interests and questions of children have no relevance to what they are required to learn in the classroom. Teachers continue to teach subject matter, not children. Any reform effort that does not confront these two issues and the changes they suggest is doomed.

This is not a scholarly book in the sense that I felt obliged to buttress my conclusions by reviewing the literature, showing where ideas came from, and refraining from taking stands (except tentatively) where the empirical evidence is scanty or absent. Anyone familiar with the literature will know that I am in debt to many people. I do wish to acknowledge my gratitude to Ed Meyer for his friendship and help during the writing of this book. This book is a personal statement requiring a personal format. That is not an apology. Form follows function.

*New Haven*                                              Seymour B. Sarason
*August 1990*

# The Author

SEYMOUR B. SARASON IS PROFESSOR OF PSYCHOLOGY EMERITUS IN the department of psychology and at the Institution for Social and Policy Studies at Yale University. He founded, in 1962, and directed, until 1970, the Yale Psycho-Educational Clinic, one of the first research and training sites in community psychology. He received his Ph.D. from Clark University in 1942 and holds honorary doctorates from Syracuse University, Queens College, and Rhode Island College. He has received an award for distinguished contributions to the public interest and several awards from the divisions of clinical and community psychology of the American Psychological Association, as well as two awards from the American Association on Mental Deficiency.

Sarason is the author of numerous books and articles. His more recent books include *The Challenge of Art to Psychology* (1990), *The Making of an American Psychologist: An Autobiography*

(1988), and *Caring and Compassion in Clinical Practice: Issues in the Selection, Training, and Behavior of Helping Professionals* (1985). He has made contributions in such fields as mental retardation, culture and personality, projective techniques, teacher training, the school culture, and anxiety in children.

**THE
PREDICTABLE
FAILURE
OF
EDUCATIONAL
REFORM**

# 1

# CONFRONTING
# INTRACTABILITY

THE TITLE OF THIS BOOK REQUIRES A BRIEF INITIAL EXPLANATION, if only to disabuse the reader of the idea that I am suggesting that we give up on reforming our schools, forget them, cut our losses, and pray that they do not get worse than they are. There are those who feel that way—although they do not say that publicly—but I regard such conclusions as at best irresponsible and at worst nihilistic. What has happened and will happen in our schools is fateful for our society. I also believe it is fateful for the world, given our country's role in it and its pervasive influences, positive and negative, on that world. What happens here is a difference that makes a difference in this world. There is more to it than that, however, and that is the fundamental question: How can we liberate the human mind to use its capacities in ways that are productively expressive of those capacities at the same time that they strengthen a sense of community? That may sound to some like high-blown rhetoric, or do-good utopianism, or unrealistic idealism. Why climb Mount Everest? Because it is there, answers the mountain climber. Analogously, in regard to the growth of the mind, we should set our goals high, very high, because we know that most peo-

1

ple are capable of more than they do or are. Unlike Mount Everest, which *can* be scaled, we can safely assume that our idealistic goals for education will not be met for everyone. But that is no warrant for starting out with modest goals that further the chances that the self-fulfilling prophecy will again be unfortunately confirmed.

The fact is that what I have just said is in no way contradicted by the rhetoric of educational reform. Have you heard anyone say that it is *not* the goal of education to enable every child "to realize his or her potential" or deny that "a wasted mind is an individual and social tragedy" or assert that we do not "owe" children the best of what we know or can do? Why call this rhetoric empty? If this is but empty rhetoric, how do we explain all of the past efforts to improve our schools? Were these efforts token gestures intended to ensure that the more things change the more they should *not* change? Was (is) there a grand conspiracy to seal over unpleasant messes, an unwillingness to give life to the rhetoric? Of course not (with the usual exceptions). I attribute to the proponents of these efforts a sincerity I would want my efforts to be accorded. They were and are no less idealistic than I am. I regard their rhetoric as empty for one reason: they have been and still are unable to explain, really to confront, two things: the deterioration in the accomplishments of our schools and the *intractability* of our schools with respect to reform efforts. It is the failure to confront goals with the realities over time that show pronouncements of Mount Everest goals to be rituals devoid of meaning and unrelated to the realities.

In the fall of 1989 an unusual event occurred, one that has taken place only twice before in the history of this country. President Bush convened a meeting of all state governors to discuss educational reform, really to begin a process of interaction between federal and state governments. In his campaign for the presidency, Mr. Bush had said that he wanted to be the "education president." Some people criticized the meeting— held on the campus of the University of Virginia, which was designed and beloved by the truly first "education president,"

Thomas Jefferson—on the grounds that it was motivated as much by political-publicity considerations as by a sense of urgency and crisis. I assume that there is a kernel of truth to the criticism. President Bush is a politician, a word I do not use pejoratively. But I also assume that he knows, and that his educational staff has told him, that the deteriorating quality of our schools has become an albatross to our society, now and for the future. The criticism is, however, clearly unwarranted for the governors, many of whom, long before the meeting, were spearheading reform efforts. Just as teachers and other personnel are near or on the firing line where the action is, the governors are nearer the action than the president.

The empty rhetoric was predictably in evidence at the meeting. Many proposals surfaced—for example, the need for a national policy, national standards of educational achievement, and higher standards for certifying educational personnel. As best as I can determine from reading accounts of the meeting and seeing parts of it on television, there were two agreed-upon implicit assumptions: The patient is sick, getting worse, but still capable of recovery; money is not the only or primary mode of treatment—that is, additional funding may or will be required but funding is not the answer. Apparently, no one saw fit to ask why, in light of the fact that in the post-World War II era we have poured scores of billions of dollars into our schools, do we have little or nothing to show for it? Granted that we could or should have spent more, should we not have expected more positive results so that this kind of meeting would not have been so necessary? Why have our efforts—and they were many and expensive—met with intractability? Why should we expect that what we will now recommend will be any more effective than our past efforts? Because of its failure to ask and confront these questions, the well-intentioned rhetoric is empty. Hope may spring eternal even though it may be powered by a repetition compulsion. Compulsive behavior is not noted for its rationality or its relationship to reality.

Let me explain what I mean by intractability by first listing the usual aims of educational reform. The aims are not discrete but overlapping. Although I have put them the way I think them, they do not do violence to what is contained in the usual rhetoric.

1.  To lessen the wide gulf between the educational accomplishments of children of different social-class and racial backgrounds.
2.  To get students to experience schooling as a process to which they are willingly attracted, not a compulsory one they see as confining and boring.
3.  To enable students to acquire knowledge and skills that are not the consequences of rote learning or of memory of abstractions devoid of personal experience but rather acquired in a way that interrelates and gives personal purpose to present and future.
4.  To engender interest in and curiosity about human accomplishments, past and present. To get students to want to know how the present contains the past—that is, to want to know this as a way of enlarging a personal, social, and "citizen" identity.
5.  To acquaint students with the domain of career options and how schooling relates to these options in a fast-changing world of work.

I shall return to aims in a later chapter. The point here is that, generally speaking, these goals have not been met despite all the efforts at educational reform. I say "generally speaking" because you can always find instances in which these goals have been approximated. But whatever lessons have been drawn from these isolated instances, they have not been successfully applied and institutionalized elsewhere. When I say that schools have been intractable to reform, I mean that for the large majority of students, including most from nonpoverty backgrounds, the declared aims of schooling are empty rhetoric that bears little relationship to their social experience. Further, I mean that the failure of educational reform derives from a most superficial conception of how complicated settings are organized: their structure, their dynamics, their power relationships, and their underlying values and axioms. Schools today are not what they were twenty or thirty years ago. They have changed but in the spirit of the popular song containing the line "I am true to you in *my* fashion", which means that the changes are cosmetic and not fundamental. Schools will remain intractable to desired reform as long as we avoid confronting (among other things) their existing power relationships, about which I will have much to say in later chapters. Avoiding those relationships is precisely what educational reformers have done, thus ensuring that the more things change, the more they will remain the same. This does not mean that if you change power relationships, desired outcomes will be achieved. It is not that simple. Changing existing power relationships is a necessary condition for reaching goals, but it is not sufficient. I shall argue that schools are distinctive but by no means unique as complicated organizations. Insofar as changing them is concerned, they are no different in their response to change than other complicated settings. As I shall attempt to show, there are some compelling and instructive nonschool examples of system change that illustrate how changing power relationships is a precondition for achieving desired outcomes. If the examples are few in number, it is because altering power relationships requires a degree of insight, vision, and courage that is in short supply among leaders of complicated organizations.

Within the past few years the issue of power relationships in school systems has been raised, and there are cases in which it has been taken seriously in practice. Although the issue has generated a good deal of discussion, that should not obscure the fact that the instances in which it has been taken seriously are truly minuscule in number. There is no ground swell, no welcome mat. Two things are troubling about these instances: they are being promoted as if there is no question about outcomes, and there seems to be no awareness that to alter the power status of teachers and parents, however necessary and desirable (and problematic), without altering power relationships *in the classroom,* is to limit drastically the chances of improving educational outcomes. Nevertheless, the fact that the question of altering power relationships has been raised, however narrowly, has to be viewed as a positive step, although the number of school systems that have gone the route of implementation is pitifully small.

This book is intended as a way of understanding intractability, the assumption being that achieving a better understanding is initially the most crucial and potentially productive factor. Inevitably, my analysis will suggest courses of action, but on a very general level. These pages will not provide a prescription for action. Further, I must warn the reader that the scope of my analysis is narrow, as I wished to emphasize only those issues too frequently ignored. Thus, I touch only lightly on the relationship between schools and university programs for the training and education of school personnel, and then only in regard to existing power relationships. I have discussed those relationships in previous books (1973; 1983; 1983; 1986; 1988, with Davidson and Blatt), and did not wish to rehash them here. Suffice it to say, these programs—their intellectual substance, the nature, length, and scope of field experience, their criteria for selection and credentialing—in all respects contain the same issues that make for controversy about how to educate children in the classrooms of our schools.

The proposal that we move, formally or informally, to national standards for student achievement, teacher competency, and school performance has a long history but has received more serious discussion in recent years. How, the argument runs, can one expect that the quality of education will improve when we have thousands of autonomous school districts differing widely and wildly on many dimensions? (This is akin to Charles de Gaulle's comment about governing France: "How can you govern a country that makes five hundred different cheeses?") Is it not time to forge national criteria of excellence to which all school districts would or should aspire? Although it is understandable why such proposals get made—reflecting as they do a response to the intractability of the bulk of autonomous school districts to demonstrate improvement—they are examples of two things: missing the point and ignoring the obvious. The obvious they ignore is the point that John Goodlad (1984) makes in his heroic study of public schools: despite the many and obvious ways in which schools differ, they are amazingly similar in terms of classroom organization, atmosphere, and rationale for learning. The point they miss is that the classroom, and the school and school system generally, are not comprehensible unless you flush out the power relationships that inform and control the behavior of everyone in these settings. Ignore those relationships, leave unexamined their rationale, and the existing "system" will defeat efforts at reform. This will happen not because there is a grand conspiracy or because of mulish stubbornness in resisting change or because educators are uniquely unimaginative or uncreative (which they are not) but rather because recognizing and trying to change power relationships, especially in complicated, traditional institutions, is among the most complex tasks human beings can undertake. The first step, recognition of the problem, is the most difficult, especially in regard to schools, because we all have been socialized most effectively to accept the power relationships characteristic of our schools as right, natural, and proper, outcomes to the contrary notwithstanding. That is why in this book I discuss the parallels between the perceived inadequacies of our schools and the growing dissatisfaction with private-sector organizations—that is, their decline in quality of product and competition. In both arenas the acceptance of existing power relationships has been disastrous. In drawing these parallels, I hope to disabuse the reader of the belief that the core problems in education are unique. They are different, not unique. In saying that, I cannot refrain from noting one respect in which our schools and society are unique, a point that is as obvious as it is grievously ignored or simply not taken seriously. We are all familiar with studies that demonstrate that, in terms of student achievement, the United States is significantly poorer than many other countries, such as Japan and Korea. These disconcerting findings, we are told, are proof positive that our schools are inadequate and in need of overhaul. Because these other countries have powerful, centralized, national standards and programs, such findings are used by some in this country to support proposals that we go down that road (just as there are some who argue similarly for a stronger federal role to stem the international decline of our private sector). It is both inexplicable and discouraging that discussion of these findings has virtually ignored the fact that the United States is unique in this world in the racial-ethnic-cultural composition of its population, a heterogeneity that in the past and present has no precedent. Indeed, in light of this fantastic heterogeneity one might seek to explain not why schools are as bad as they are but rather why they are as good as they are. It may be true that no country in human history has ever had anything resembling our immigration experience. I do not, however, offer these conclusions as an excuse, let alone a justification, for our educational ills, or as an argument for inaction. They are conclusions that indicate again how difficult it is to take the obvious seriously.

If in the following chapters I adopt what some may perceive as a narrow perspective from which to view educational reform, I have to plead guilty. My defense is that in restricting myself to issues of power relationships, I am addressing issues that, if left unexplored and undiscussed, will limit drastically the desirable outcomes sought by any effort on any educational problem. For those who find themselves agreeing with my argument, I need to stress that changing power relationships is no guarantee that those alterations will lead to improvement in educational outcomes. One seeks those alterations because one has a special vision about what people are and can be. To confuse change with progress is to confuse means with ends. Keeping those ends in mind, informing as they should the means in the most pervasive ways, is a responsibility that too often fades into the background in the turmoil of change. The means become ends in themselves and, therefore, the more things change the more they remain the same, or worse. It is the rare revolution that has been true to its initial vision.

# 2

## CONCEPTUALIZING THE EDUCATIONAL SYSTEM

I WAS VISITED IN 1989 BY A YOUNG FRIEND WHO RETURNED TO New Haven for the twentieth reunion of his graduating class at Yale. When I got to know him in the sizzling sixties, I initially regarded him as another one of those radical activists with a bottomless capacity for oversimplification of issues. That was not a pejorative judgment, because the issues he and his cohort posed were important, their moral indignation understandable and admirable, and their sincerity unquestionable. To me, however, their diagnoses were egregiously superficial and their solutions the hallmark of how little they understood their society and how it works. But, I soon learned, my young friend was refreshingly different from most other students in two respects. For one thing, you could argue with him. He had a capacity to listen: he truly tried to understand our differences in views. He did not regard me and a few other of his teachers as archconservatives erecting barricades against social progress. Although his views did not change much, if at all, as a result of our arguments, I felt that there was a part of him that could take distance from his thoughts and actions—that is, he could reflect. The other respect in which he differed from almost all of his Yale cohort was his decision to make a career in public education because, he had decided, that is where he could make a difference. This was a young man who, in terms of level of ability, potential for high-level conceptualization, leadership qualities, and personal attractiveness and sense of humor, would probably have been successful in any line of endeavor that he chose.

He made it his business to stay in touch with me. He became a teacher, got his credentials as a principal, and was a principal for several years until he started a small educational consulting firm. Whenever we met, I was impressed not only with what he was doing but also with his need to put his experience in some kind of framework. He is a reader, and a rather voracious one. Several years ago he and I jointly led a seminar at a small private teachers college on policy issues in education. He organized the year-long seminar, brought in several very stimulating speakers, and in the discussions demonstrated a capacity to get at the heart of matters. He was still the activist, still committed to making a difference, but there was now a note of skepticism-pessimism in his outlook.

In the first fifteen minutes of our meeting, the young man (he was now in his early forties!) described the experiences he had had and was having in his work in urban schools around the country. It was fascinating fare he related with enthusiasm, even though to me it was a litany of good intentions colliding with intractable problems. At one point I asked him: "What keeps you going? I admire what you are trying to do, but from your own account you are like Sisyphus pushing a big boulder up the hill only to see it slide back to the bottom. What keeps you going?" A puzzled frown appeared fleetingly on his face before he replied: "It is interesting that you should ask me that question because I have been struggling with it. I have come to the conclusion that the next ten years are crucial for our society and the world. More specifically, unless in the next ten years we make real progress about educational reform, the downward societal slide will continue, and when I think about my daughter and her future I get scared. And I have also concluded that it is my generation that has to do that job because those who came before us failed and those who come after us will not or cannot. We are the only hope."

We looked at each other rather intently. My reaction must have registered on my face because he then said to me, in a tentative somewhat anxious voice, "You think it is hopeless, don't you?" I was surprised to hear myself say yes because I had never verbalized that answer to anyone before. He had to leave for the reunion festivities and remarked in parting: "Please don't give up hope."

For the rest of that day I reflected on my answer. I realized that I had come to that answer long before articulating it to my friend. If that answer stayed within me, it was because I did not want to be perceived as an old fogey who overgeneralized from his own inadequacies in thinking and action. The truth is that I was bothered by my sense of hopelessness not because I doubted my conclusion but because it engendered a sense of intellectual loneliness—that is, there was something I believed that I could not talk about to others. I anticipated that if I said what I believed, I would be viewed as kin to those who proclaim that the end of the world is near.

The conversation with my young friend was but one stimulus to putting my argument in order. No less influential were conversations I had and was having with people at all levels of the educational hierarchy, as well as with university faculty involved in public education. Each of these conversations was with one other person. This is significant because what many of these people were saying in a private, face-to-face interchange was different from what they were saying publicly. (That was as true for me as it was for them.) And these people were saying clearly that the efforts to improve educational outcomes had been and would be failures. Their reasons were by no means uniform; the only thing upon which they agreed was that none of the efforts of which they had been part to improve education generally had had any positive effects. Several of them had spent decades spearheading educational reform.

There were a few others with whom I talked who had not yet succumbed to what some would call defeatism. If they were not defeatist, they were clearly not optimistic. They were puzzled, resigned, and searching for an explanation that would justify hope. Interestingly, these educators said—more correctly, implied—that they did not use the size of school budgets as an excuse for the large number of school dropouts and pallid school achievement scores. And although they were gratified that the salaries of educational personnel had increased discernibly and justifiably, none of them expected, as a consequence, that the achievement scores would noticeably increase. As one of these administrators said: "When you think of it, it is grossly insulting to say that if you pay educators more they will put out more and educational outcomes will markedly increase. How demeaning it is to suggest that those who are in the trenches hold back their fire and deliberately do less than they can or should."

The origins of my dysphoric response go back a long way. For almost half a century I have witnessed and have been a participant in efforts generally to improve our educational systems. For much of that time, and in very diverse forums, I advocated for this or that kind of change, always assuming that what I recommended would, if appropriately implemented, have the desired effects. And what I recommended went far beyond helping individual teachers or changing a single school. I had demonstrated to my satisfaction, and to that of others, that such important but narrow goals were achievable if certain conditions existed. But precisely because such conditions were infrequent—and even when they were met, sustaining the desired changes was by no means assured—I came to see what should have been obvious: the characteristics, traditions, and organizational dynamics of school systems were more or less lethal obstacles to achieving even modest, narrow goals. How does one deal with the abstraction we call a system embedded in and reflective of a society that created and nurtured that system? Can such a system be altered from within? Does it require changes and pressures from without, or does it require some kind of transactional readiness from both sources? And how do we determine whether we are tinkering with and even bolstering the system rather than changing it? And what do we mean by educational system? Do we mean how people are se-

lected to enter the system? How, once selected, they are prepared to be in the system? In what relation do they stand to
decision-making forums that affect them? And can one conceptualize the system apart from its relations to the political
system and its decision-making processes, formal and informal? Are parents and others part of the system? And can one
think of the system without students: their developmental
characteristics, their assigned roles, their perception of the system and their roles in it?

It is noteworthy, indeed symptomatic, that the proponents
of educational reform do not talk about changing the educational system. They will couch their reforms in terms of improving schools or the quality of education. And if there is any
doubt that they have other than the most superficial conception of the educational system, that doubt disappears when one
examines their remedies, which add up to "we will do what we
have been doing, or what we ought to be doing, only we will
now do it better." In the past decade there have been scores of
reports—by presidential and gubernatorial commissions, by
foundation task forces—about how to improve educational
outcomes. I have read most of them (for insomniacs they are
far more effective than barbiturates) and none of them addresses interrelated questions: In what ways do our recommendations differ from those made by comparable groups
twenty or even fifty years ago? How do we account for what
seems to be the universal conclusion that there has been a
marked deterioration in the climate and accomplishments of
our schools? Why should the solutions we offer make a difference? If these questions were not raised in the reports, it is not
because they were not discussed among those who wrote them.
In talking to these commission members, as I have, one is struck
by two facts. First, they think they know who the villains are:
inadequate teachers, irresponsible parents, irrelevant or inadequate curricula, unmotivated students from whom too little is
expected or demanded, an improvement-defeating bureaucracy, a lowering of standards for promotion and graduation,
and a lack of competitiveness that would serve as a goad for
schools to take steps to improve themselves. I use the word

*villain* advisedly because the assignment of blame allows them to pinpoint their recommendations for change. In a truly basic way they indict the motivations of this or that group or practice, as if current conditions were willed. It is no wonder that implied in their recommendations is a "shape up or ship out" attitude. Someone once said that it is hard to be completely wrong, and that is the case with these commission reports. There are kernels of truth in their criticisms but these have been identified before and have led to actions that were obviously ineffective. Why should similar diagnoses and actions today be more effective?

The second striking fact one learns from talking with those who wrote and sanctioned these reports is that they accept the system as it is. Whatever changes they seek to make do not require altering the nature of the relationships among those who make up the system. I am reminded here of a discussion I had a couple of decades ago with an executive of a foundation that was pouring a great deal of money into New Haven generally and the school system in particular. After one of his visits, he told me that he was unimpressed with the pace, direction, and effectiveness of the efforts at reform in the New Haven schools. I asked him, "If you could do what you wanted in the New Haven schools, where would you start?" He answered, "I would send all of the school principals to Mexico City to a two-year convention." Change the personnel and improvement will follow! He did not want to change the role of the principal in regard to other roles or participants in the system; he wanted to select principals who could "think," who would adapt to new circumstances. It did not occur to him that the principals he derogated, almost all of whom he had never met, might once have been thinking people imbued with a sense of missionary zeal that had been extinguished by a variety of features of the system. Why over time should new principals not experience the same fate? Here, too, one could say that this foundation executive was not completely wrong in that some of the principals he found wanting or incompetent deserved criticism, and even removal. But he was egregiously wrong in suggesting that the inadequacies were due only to their personality make up, and in no way reflected the effects over time of the system on those within it. I am not excusing ineffectiveness, incompetence, or mediocrity. But when one concludes that almost all people in a particular role are inadequate, should one not ask what there is about the system that makes or sustains such failures in performance? And if that question is not asked, how can one assume that the new cadre of principals will not experience the same fate?

One can see, touch, and interact with people and things, but not with the abstraction we call a system. System is a concept we create to enable us to indicate that in order to understand a part we have to study it in relation to other parts. It would be more correct to say that when we use the concept *system* it refers to the existence of parts, that those parts stand in diverse relationships to each other, and that between and among those parts are boundaries (another abstraction) of varying strength and permeability. Between system and surround are also boundaries, and trying to change any part of the system requires knowledge and understanding of how parts are interrelated. At the very least, taking the concept of system seriously is a control against overly simple cause-and-effect explanations and interventions that are based on tunnel vision.

When you read the myriad of recommendations these commission reports contain, it becomes clear that they are not informed by any conception of a system. That is a charitable assessment. It deserves emphasis that none of these reports confronts the question of why these recommendations for changing this or that part of the system, which have been made in the past, have been ineffective. More upsetting is the question of why so many people think the situation has not remained the same but has deteriorated. Why, in the quiet of the night, do so many people think that the situation is hopeless?

The reader may find it helpful to engage in the following exercise. Imagine a situation where you are empowered to initiate one change, and only one, in a school system. There is but one restriction: the change cannot cost discernibly more money than is now available. What would that change be and why would you choose that one from the universe of alternatives? If you start with some conception of the nature of a school system, you will not quickly arrive at an answer because there is, one can safely assume, a surfeit of changes you deem necessary. But, as you can make only one change, on what basis should your decision rest? Obviously, you will seek that change which, if appropriately implemented (quite an assumption!), will have over time desirable percolating effects on other problems in other parts of the system. The important point is that you do not choose a change because it addresses an important problem—of which there are many—but because what you seek to change is so embedded in a system of interacting parts that if it is changed, then changes elsewhere are likely to occur.

The kind of thinking this exercise requires clearly did not inform the scores of commission reports written in the past decades. The reasons are many, not the least of which is that we are not used to or comfortable with thinking in terms of systems. It is a difficult and humbling way of thinking because you quickly come to see the complexity you are trying to understand and how little you know about how its parts transact with each other. And if you discuss your understandings with others struggling with the same task, it becomes clear that this thing we call a school system engenders reactions no less diverse than those to an ink blot. And if that diversity is small, or even nonexistent, the chances are extremely high that there will be disagreement about what would be the most productive changes with which to start.

There is, however, a problem prior to thinking in terms of a system. How does one come to know a system—to have those experiences with it that will act as a control against overly simplified conceptualizing, the drawing of unrevealing diagrams and charts, and parochialism of outlook and roles? Almost all of the people who have served on these commissions have no first-hand experience in school systems, apart from having been students when they were young albeit in a somewhat different world than that of today. Although one should not write off such prior experience as useless, conclusions drawn from it are hardly a basis for recommending actions. These commission members—chosen for their accomplishments and status in diverse areas, testifying presumably to a capacity to get at the heart of issues in areas with which they are unfamiliar—lack the experience in education that would enable them to begin to think in terms of a system. I am not being disrespectful or ungrateful or demeaning. I am saying what I think is a brute fact: almost all of these people have no experiential basis for the task they were asked to accept. It can be rightfully argued, of course, that these commission members are not chosen for their expertise in education but rather for the clout their names and status lend to reports developed and written by a staff that does contain individuals whose credentials are in education. These individuals, frequently from the university, are almost always not part of an ongoing school system, however, although some in the past have had a role in it.

I am not arguing that if you have not had experience in schools in the past two decades, you should remain silent. To make that point clear, let me relate a conversation with a business executive who was part of a local task force to improve the school system. He had taken over a company that was on the verge of bankruptcy and over a period of five years had transformed it into a very profitable enterprise. I had been invited to a task force meeting, during which it became clear that he was committed to public education; he was dismayed, to say the least, at the inadequacies of the local schools; he was convinced that the schools required more firm leadership, a more explicit statement of goals, and more systematic processes of accountability. It is correct to say that the management aspects of running our schools was his central recommendation—that is, he recommended that principles of effective management in the private sector should be applied to the schools.

I sought him out after the meeting and had a long talk with him. Part of the conversation went like this (reconstructed):

*SBS:* Let us imagine that a new superintendent has just been chosen and he or she comes to you for advice. What are some of the things you would say to this person?

*CEO:*   That is a hard question and I could not be specific in answering. I think I know in a general way what I would advise but I don't know that that would be helpful. After all, I am not an educator.

*SBS:*   What would some of these generalizations be?

*CEO:*   Well, the first thing I would advise is that he or she articulate specific goals that are concrete, comprehensible, and would receive general agreement. For example, one such goal would be a reduction in absenteeism of students and staff. Who are these absentees? How quickly are those with the most frequent absences identified and who follows them up and how quickly are they helped to be where they are supposed to be? You don't collect such data at the end of a school year or every few months, long after a pattern has been established. You develop procedures that tell you or your staff quickly what is going on in these respects and require you to take remedial action.

*SBS:*   That makes sense. What about another generalization that should lead to action?

*CEO:*   What I am going to say now is touchy and truly is the test of leadership: you have to institute ways of evaluating the competency of your administrative staff to do what they are supposed to do. And that is also true for the teachers they supervise. In fact, I would tell the superintendent if at the end of the first year, you have not gotten rid of any employee, teacher or staff, or if the number is very small, something is wrong. Given what we know about this school system, and I have heard no one say that it is other than inadequate, it seems obvious that more than a handful of people should not be in the system. I would tell him or her that I am not advocating a witch hunt but an adherence to standards that must be met. If the superintendent waffles in these matters, that person is not doing his or her job.

*SBS:*   What about one more piece of advice?

*CEO:*   I suppose I should say what is obvious but rarely taken seriously by school systems, this one at least. There is a budget and you have to stay within it, a fact that should be made clear to everyone. It would be nice, of course, if the budget could be larger but that is not in the cards, given the nature of the economy of this city. There is a bottom line and that is fiscal responsibility.

*SBS:* May I shift the direction of our conversation? I know that several years ago you took over your company, which was near bankruptcy. Today it is thriving and growing. Why did you buy this company? More specifically, what experience did you have with the manufacture of the products they made?

*CEO:* I knew very little in a technical sense about their manufacturing process. I, like you I assume, knew their products, which had enjoyed quite a good reputation before they began the downhill slide. When I studied the situation—their financial sheets, conversations with some of their executives and managers—I decided that I could turn things around.

*SBS:* When you took over, what was your game plan? What were the *predictable* problems you would have to confront?

*CEO:* I am not sure I know what you mean. Obviously, I and the staff I brought with me would have to find out where the problems were. And by problems I mean people, departments, and processes. Some of the problems we knew, others we would have to discover.

*SBS:* Let me ask it in another way. What thought, if any, did you give to how people in the organization would view you?

*CEO:* I see what you mean. I expected two reactions: one was relief that new life would be breathed into the organization, and the other was fear that heads would roll, divisions would be eliminated, and all kinds of changes would be required.

*SBS:* Did that worry you?

*CEO:* It sure as hell did because those fears were not only real but if I didn't address them the situation could deteriorate quickly and really got out of hand.

*SBS:*   So what did you do?

*CEO:*   I spent one day drafting a two-page letter that went to everyone, but everyone. In it I told them that I knew how they felt and that they had reason to be concerned. But I also said that no quick action was planned. I outlined a plan by which people at different levels would meet among themselves and come up with recommendations about how the company could be improved. No one would sign their name to the report which would come to me. And what I emphasized was that I was serious about getting their recommendations.

*SBS:*   What reason did you have to think that they would believe you?

*CEO:*   I knew they wanted to believe me but that that belief was surrounded by doubt and fear. Look, I came up the hard and long way. I have worked at every level of a manufacturing company. I have seen companies from the bottom, the middle, and the top. And I am not patting myself on the back when I say I know how rank-and-file people see things. In fact, for a week after we came on the scene, I and my staff visited and discussed my letter with each division and arranged for them to meet several times for one hour. The message we conveyed was that we wanted to be judged by what we would do and not what we had said. We were not giving them "released time" as a sop as they went to the guillotine.

*SBS:*   That strikes me as unusual thinking and action.

*CEO:*   Maybe it is. But I have learned, and it pays off, I can assure you, that in these situations my self-preservation requires good morale in others. You not only have to listen, but you have to *hear* what people are saying and feeling, and you have to feel respect for them even though they are not telling you what you want to hear. That letter was only the first step in demonstrating *in action* that I would try never to act unilaterally.

*SBS:*   It sounds as if you spend as much time listening as talking.

*CEO:*   I spend more time listening.

*SBS:*   Can you tell me briefly what you expected from these initial reports?

*CEO:*   (Laughing). Two things. The first is that I would learn a lot about what people at different levels in different divisions perceived to be important problems. The second, and the reason I laughed, is that I expected that people at a particular level would in some way see those below them as a source of problems. Not always, of course, because I expected that in a few instances those above them would be blamed. But in general I expected, and was right, that blame is downward assigned. Except, of course, for those at the bottom of the pyramid who can only assign blame upward. That is what I call standardized operating procedure for assigning blame and coming up smelling roses.

*SBS:*   Are you saying that you cannot understand one part of the organization apart from the others? That problems are never self-contained? That it is truly a system of interlocking, interacting parts?

*CEO:*   Isn't that obvious? You had better believe it.

*SBS:*   One more question along these lines. Once you decided what the problems were and what needed to be done, what did you expect would happen?

*CEO:*   I am not sure I know what you mean. One thing I knew for certain was that the big problems were ahead of me.

*SBS:*   Now I am not sure what you mean.

*CEO:*   To say it the way I thought it: I knew that when the changes were announced, it would be an example of the shit hitting the fan. Things were going to change and who, in these situations, likes change? In fact, I wrote another letter that went to everyone explaining the changes and saying in bold print that I knew that change was never easy and I sought their understanding, patience, and cooperation.

*SBS:*   You expected resistance, in some quarters at least?

*CEO:*   Of course. If I didn't know that, if the staff I brought with me didn't know it, we could be dead ducks. *I* owned the company but my fate was ultimately in their hands, which means everyone else in the company. Let me be clear on that point: I was never in doubt, and I made sure no one else was in doubt, about who would make final decisions. But I made it clear that no decisions would be made unilaterally—that is, without people feeling that they had had a hearing or that I or my staff had listened and discussed matters with them.

*SBS:*   From what people have told me, things went well.

*CEO:*   They went well but not easily, then or now. (Teasingly). But I haven't told you my ace in the hole.

*SBS:*   What was that?

*CEO:*   I instituted a profit-sharing plan. If I win, they win.

*SBS:*   It is getting late and I have to get back to New Haven. So let me put to you one more question that has bothered me in our conversation. It is less a question than it is a kind of paradox and I hope you will not take it as criticism. When I asked you earlier about the advice you would give to a new superintendent of schools, you articulated what I consider to be some superficial generalizations which in no way indicated that you had any usable knowledge about how hierarchically organized, complex human systems work and how they are experienced by those within them. But when you talked about how you went about changing a deteriorating complex organization—how you thought, the values you hold, your sensitivity to how people experience and can be adversely affected by a system, the obstacles to *and* the opportunities for change—a picture emerged that in no way informed what you said to a new superintendent taking over your schools.

*CEO:*   You mean I know much more about school systems than I give myself credit for?

*SBS:*   *That* you had better believe.

*CEO:* (Laughing). Are you saying that I should or could be a superintendent of schools?

*SBS:* Yes and no. The answer is definitely no if your question implies that heads of large private businesses think and act the way you do. I have met and talked with many chief executive officers and very few have your style of thinking and acting, which is one reason our private sector has been steadily losing ground in terms of quality, efficiency, and competitiveness. They would advise a new superintendent the way you initially did. Indeed, in terms of style of thinking and acting, and the values that undergird them, superintendents and their "management staff" are more like than unlike private business executives. The answer is yes in *your* case if only because you strike me as someone with that rare capacity to transfer knowledge appropriately from one realm of experience to another, even if those realms seem to be wildly dissimilar. They are different in very important and crucial ways but far from totally different.

*CEO:* You don't sound optimistic about improving our schools. If what you say about superintendents is true—and intuitively I think you are right about them and my counterparts in the private sector—we are really in trouble.

*SBS:* I am the opposite of optimistic. But I do not want to scapegoat superintendents. They came up in the system and they are products of it. Like your counterparts, they are, with few exceptions, bright, well-intentioned, hard-working people. But they are products of a system and they are imprisoned in it. There are some exceptions.

*CEO:* I must confess that ever since I agreed to serve on this and that task force or committee having to do with the school system—and reluctantly had to decline nomination to the school board—I would occasionally entertain the thought that I could make a good superintendent.

*SBS:* I think you would, not because you are a successful businessman but because of several other factors: you have an articulated but sophisticated understanding of complex organizations; you are sensitive to what happens to and among people in a hierarchy; you are respectful of their attitudes and needs; and you seem to believe that anyone who will be affected by change should stand in some relationship to the formulation and implementation of that change.

*CEO:*    Thanks for the compliments. I never would have described myself that way. Whenever I am asked to account for my success—and I find that a very embarrassing question I do not like to be asked—I say two things: I learn from my mistakes and I have no difficulty owning up to them quickly and publicly.

I have no doubt that if this unusual man had been on a presidential or governor's commission to make recommendations for improving schools, he would heartily have approved and signed a report that in no way reflected his experience in a complex human system. In his own bailiwick, he had a comprehensive conception of a system. Sitting on a task force, he saw only unconnected parts. Having little or no hands-on experience in schools is a very serious limitation on those with the responsibility to make recommendations for improving them. Ignorance is no virtue. It is, in this case, a mammoth obstacle because it reinforces the misconception that schools are not complex systems having many of the features of other types of complex systems. It is one thing to say that school systems are different, it is quite another to say they are unique. Having read scads of commission reports, I can only conclude that they rest on the invalid assumption that school systems are unique systems.

The reader should not conclude that I believe that educational reform should be left to educators—that is, that they possess a sophisticated conception of schools as systems. Teachers, principals, supervisors, curriculum specialists, superintendents, members of boards of education—with rare exceptions, those who belong to these groups think and perceive in terms of parts and not a complicated system: *their* parts, *their* tasks, *their* problems, *their* power or lack of it. If there is any doubt about this, one should pose, as I have, a specific problem or issue to each of these groups for their recommendations. The responses are so varied, often so conflicting, that one might conclude that a school system seems for its members to have the features of an ink blot. Of course, each group knows that there is a "system" but each sees it from a particular perspective which, by its narrowness, precludes understanding of any other perspective. One might expect, for example, that those in administrative positions, each of whom had occupied lower-level positions (as teachers), would in their recommendations indicate a sensitivity to and comprehension of those below them—that is, one would expect a discernible degree of overlap in their perspectives. That is rarely the case. Predictably, they see themselves as adversaries. They literally do not understand each other, and by understand I mean being able to comprehend, to try to comprehend, how and why people in different roles see matters so differently, how and why the system engenders and sustains such radical differences in perspective, and why explanations of these differences in terms of "personality" contain but a small kernel of truth.

I have been in the habit, whenever I have met with educators in a system and it appeared opportune, of asking them why adversarial attitudes and stands are predictable features of a school system: a mini United Nations in which the pursuit of narrow self-interest is all-pervasive. I take pains to point out that I do not hold the utopian view that it is possible to have a complex social system in which intergroup conflict is truly minimal, let alone absent. But why, I ask, is the level of adversarialism in school systems, especially urban ones, not only such a conspicuous feature but seemingly so self-defeating of everyone's goals? When taken together, the replies add up to a litany of blame assigned to those above or below the particular group's role level, mostly below.

The adversarial stance is not only a feature of the encapsulated school system. For example, on numerous occasions when I have met with a group of teachers over time, I have said to them: "From our previous discussions I want to pose a question to which I think I know the answer. Imagine that you have to choose one of these alternatives: you get a sizable salary increase or you will not be required ever to talk to and meet with parents. Which would you choose?" Invariably, the question elicits a kind of nervous laughter suggesting not only that an irritating problem has been exposed but also that making a choice would not be automatic. I have never asked for a formal vote because the point of the question was only to underline and discuss what someone once termed the "original cold war."

I have presented two conclusions which together explain in part why educational reform either is not attempted or is carried out in an institutional context of which the reformers have little or no knowledge. The first conclusion is that those outside the system with responsibility for articulating a program for reform have nothing resembling a holistic conception of the system they seek to influence. In principle, I have argued, that ignorance need not be lethal, although it almost always has been. The second conclusion is that being part of the system—part, so to speak, of the school culture—in no way guarantees that one understands the system in any comprehensive way. This has been an old problem for the anthropologist planning a study of foreign culture. The anthropologist knows that as a stranger, an outsider, one can make some egregious errors of omission and commission even if one has read whatever is available about that culture. (Unlike outsiders on educational task forces, the anthropologist zealously tries to learn as much as possible about the subject.) There are advantages and disadvantages to being an outsider, but the anthropologist knows that, once on the scene, the live culture will differ in striking ways from what one has learned by reading the relevant literature. The anthropologist also knows or expects that different individuals in that culture will not describe the culture in identical ways. Indeed, for some of his or her purposes, no one in the culture can provide relevant information because what is sought rests on axioms that no one in the culture has put into words. In any event, the most fateful decision the anthropologist has to make once on the scene is to determine who would be reliable informants about what the culture is, how it works, and what are its interacting parts and system characteristics. In short, the anthropologist does not want to make the mistakes that so many foreigners make when they come to study the United States, or that the United States made in its foreign aid programs after World War II. Mistakes in understanding are one thing; when they become the basis for action, it is quite another thing. In education the mistakes in conception and action have been many, and almost all of them derive from an inability to comprehend the nature of school systems. This inability prevents dealing with the question of how one decides where the change process should begin, because that is the starting point from which changes elsewhere will occur. But one cannot ask that question if one's stance is: there is problem A we have to do something about, there is problem B, there is problem C, and so on. When each problem is posed and attacked separately, when each of a number of important problems is considered equally important in terms of its system implications, the chances of failure are very high. This is not to suggest that all important problems be attacked at the same time. It is necessary but not sufficient to try to understand how these problems are interrelated and reflect the nature of the system. What is crucial is to decide which of these problems should be a starting point, because if one deals successfully, even in part, with that problem, changes elsewhere in the system are likely to occur over time. The importance of a problem is but one criterion for choosing a starting point.

There is, I have come to conclude, a ubiquitous feature of complex human systems that should inform thinking and action in regard to educational reform. It is a feature that, if not taken seriously, invites failure. This is the fact that any social system can be described in terms of power relationships. Power is distributed unequally among the members of the system, and there is always a rationale for this unequal distribution of power. Put in another way, that differential allocation of power is justified by tradition and necessity; it is a way of ensuring that the overarching goals of the system will be effectively achieved. There is not only a division of labor but also a differential assignment of power in regard to planning, policy formulation, decision making, and implementation. All of this is obvious and taken for granted until it becomes clear, as in the case of school systems, that the system is not achieving its stated goals. In the case of our schools, one would have hoped that there would be recognition of the probability that the failings of the system derive in part from the nature of existing power relationships—that this pattern of relationships is no longer adequate or appropriate. (The most inspiring and instructive example is how the constitutional convention of 1787 struggled with the issues of power in the face of the inadequacies of the power relationship contained in the earlier Articles of Confederation.) With two exceptions, the existing pattern of the distribution of power never informed the goals of and methods for change. There was nothing wrong with that pattern; the problem was defined as getting better people to use their assigned powers more effectively! The idea that the distribution of power needed to be changed was never addressed. In the plethora of commission and task force reports of the last decade, the possibility that power relationships should be altered is never raised, even if one reads between the lines. And, yet, if anything is clear from the efforts to reform our schools in the post-World War II era, the relative or total failure of these efforts can in large measure be attributed to a gross insensitivity to how power was employed in the planning and implementation of change. Any effort to deal with or prevent a significant problem in a school system that is not based on a reallocation of power—a discernible change in power relationships—is doomed. This is not to say that in and of itself a particular reallocation of power will have positive consequences, but such a change is a recognition that a feature of the system has been confronted. And if the situation is favorable in regard to implementing and sustaining such a change, that change in power relationships can have percolating effects in the system qua system.

Now for the two exceptions. One is the rise in strength and influence of teacher unions, a development that at its core sought to change existing power relationships. The other exception is Public Law 94–142, the Education of All Handicapped Children legislation of 1975, a key feature of which was to change power relationships between parents and educational decision makers. In neither case did school systems react warmly—to indulge understatement—to this threat to existing power relationships. They were, so to speak, forced to accommodate to the threat. That should not occasion surprise. People rarely embrace a restriction or alteration in the scope of their accustomed powers. If reformers have steered clear of dealing with alternatives in patterns of power relationships, it is testimony both to a reluctance to change the system and an unwillingness to confront the conflicts such changes inevitably engender. The result has been that reformers rivet on problems they can deal with and gloss over problems they often regard as more important but too controversial.

In one report sponsored by a prestigious foundation, it is recommended that teachers should have a role in decision making, on the grounds that if teachers are to be truly professional they should have more power over matters affecting their everyday practices. That recommendation received a good deal of play in the public media, and was warmly supported on the editorial pages of our national newspapers. Unlike some other recommendations in that report, which were very clear, concrete, and specific in terms of action and funding, the one about increasing the power of teachers was couched in the most general terms. What should that recommendation mean for action? What educational decision-making processes should teachers be part of? Why will such a recommendation be difficult to initiate and sustain? Why is it likely, perhaps certain, that the recommendation will go nowhere? If one is an optimist, as I am, one is grateful for small favors and therefore heartened that this power issue has been raised, albeit generally and innocuously. If one is a pessimist, as I am, one is disappointed but not surprised that the report writers refrained from pursuing in any detail why the recommendation must and will encounter an obstacle course. My pessimism was mightily increased when, on July 18, 1989, I read in the *New York Times* the following:

Citing a need for a "new image of teachers in this country," a 64-member board released guidelines yesterday for the first national system to set standards for the best teachers and to determine who meets them.

In doing so, the National Board for Professional Teaching Standards spelled out its definition of what teachers "should know and be able to do" and announced the 29 fields in which it will offer such certification.

The board was created three years ago by the Carnegie Forum on Education and the Economy to design and administer the new system, which will supplement, not replace, teacher certification by individual states. The goal is to form a national cadre of distinguished professionals who will enhance the status of teaching, raise salaries, and attract more talented people into the field . . .

The board plans to start a $50 million research effort to design new techniques, including the use of computer simulations of classroom situations, to determine who meets its standards. The first teachers are expected to be certified in 1993, when it has been predicted by education experts that the quantity and quality of American teachers will be low if nothing is done . . .

. . . national certification would become "a lever for other fundamental changes" in American schools, including changes in the management of schools to give teachers a greater role in making educational decisions. "For once in this country, we are working out standards for measuring excellence rather than minimum competence," he said.

Why national certification of teachers will become a "lever" to give teachers a greater role in making educational decisions escapes me. Why should that lever be more successful than any other? Why should it alter existing power relationships? When the recommendation about changing the role of teachers in decision making was initially made, the then secretary of education, and the national organization representing school administrators, proclaimed publicly and unambiguously that they considered the recommendation stupid and an invitation to chaos. Again, their response should occasion no surprise. Why should the creation of a National Board for Professional Teaching Standards be effective in dissolving the opposition of those who do not look gleefully at a sharing of power? I am not criticizing the creation of such a board, although part of me believes that it is another example of doing what we know how to do, not what we know needs to be done. Any educational reform that does not explicitly and courageously own up to issues surrounding changing patterns of power relationships is likely to fail. That prediction is based on the feckless consequence of educational reform in the past half-century.

# 3

# INTERNAL AND EXTERNAL
# PERSPECTIVES ON
# THE SYSTEM

IF YOU ENTER THE ARENA OF EDUCATIONAL REFORM WITH A "FIND
the villain" stance, you contribute to what is already a conceptual cloud chamber. There are no villains in the sense that this
or that group in or related to the system deliberately sought to
make a bad situation worse. Some groups have more responsibility than others for what happens, some groups resist change
more than others, and groups differ greatly on "why and how
we got into this mess" and what needs to be done to improve
the situation. Few things have contributed more to failure than
the inability to comprehend how these different groups condition each other's perspective. To focus on one part or group
in the system independent of how that group conditions and
is conditioned by other groups immediately reduces the chances
that you will achieve your goals. That, I must reiterate, does
not mean that on the level of action you have to deal with all
groups at the same time, which if theoretically desirable is in
practice impossible. It means that on the level of action you
should always be dealing with more than one group. Which
other groups you choose depends on the way you scale them
in terms of their influence on each other—and that kind of

scaling should be based on dispassionate understanding of the system, not on a rogues' gallery of targeted villains.

There are three kinds of understanding. One is about the present and near past—that is, one seeks to understand why a problem has become a problem in the here and now and the recent past. That is the most frequent kind of understanding sought. The second kind, extraordinarily infrequent and in my own experience always absent, is contained in three questions: Has this particular problem, or a similar one, occurred before in the history of this system? If it has, what was done about it with what degree of effect? What is there about the system that accounts for cyclical occurrence, if indeed the problem has been cyclical rather than constant? The first kind of understanding is based on the assumption that the problem and the system were born yesterday. The second assumes that history is always a variable, an instructive one. The former is a characteristic of almost every commission report, as if dealing with institutional history is frivolous or a luxury. The latter is the domain of a small group of historians of education, who are both highly regarded and totally unheeded. If anything characterizes educational reform in the past half-century, it has been its ahistorical stance. The significance of the historical stance is not only in what it tells us about the manifestations of a particular problem over time, or in what one learns about the efficacy of remedial actions, but also in what one learns about the system qua system—that is, the features of the system in which the problem arises and recurs, or remains constant but unremarked until it is seen (again) as destabilizing the system.

There is a third kind of understanding which relates school systems to the larger social system. In some ultimate sense, it is an understanding of how social problems, processes, and changes external to schools impinge dramatically on schools and create problems for them. At the very least, formally or informally, noticed or not, they initiate a change process in the schools. For example, the rise and relative success of the women's liberation movement dramatically changed the composition of those who sought careers in education. Similarly, the development of a vast computer industry paying salaries very much above teacher salaries drastically reduced the number of people seeking to be math teachers, and also produced a flight of math and science teachers from the classroom to private industry. The orbiting of the first Russian sputnik in 1957, the civil rights movement of the sixties and seventies, Vietnam, an increasing divorce rate and changes in family structure, deterioration of urban areas—these are a few examples of how changes in the larger society inevitably impinged on the school culture.

We are used to hearing that schools are a creation and reflection of the larger society. It is hard to quarrel with that generalization, but it glosses over more than it illuminates. For example, it does not tell us that the turmoil accompanying these social changes will also accompany the accommodations the schools seek to make. Nor does it tell us that resistance to these accommodations will be no less strong than the resistance in the larger society. Nor does it direct our attention to the different ways the schools can or should accommodate. Should this accommodation concern a curriculum change? A change in administrative structure? A reallocation of resources? A change in power relationships and decision-making processes? A change in standards? The major limitation of the generalization is that it does not alert us to a highly predictable fact: like almost all other complex traditional social organizations, the schools will accommodate in ways that require little or no change. This is not to say that the accommodation is insincere or deliberately cosmetic but rather that the strength of the status quo—its underlying axioms, its pattern of power relationships, its sense of tradition and therefore what seems right, natural, and proper—almost automatically rules out options for change in that status quo.

The three kinds of understanding briefly described are essential for comprehending any of the major problems confronting schools. No major educational problem is only a "within system" problem—that is, arising in and comprehensible only in terms of an encapsulated school culture. That should be a glimpse of the obvious requiring action that explicitly and meaningfully takes the obvious seriously. That means that any

action that stays within the system—based only on its own resources, personnel, decision-making processes, and planning—
is misconceived, parochial, and likely to fail. At the very least,
such actions have to involve and share responsibility with individuals and agencies formally unrelated to schools but formally involved with and responsible for a social problem that
manifests itself in schools. If I am right in saying that no major
educational problem is only a "within system" problem, then
attacking the problem must never be conceived as only a school
problem. But that is precisely the cage in which educational
reformers have imprisoned themselves: defining and attacking
problems in the most narrow ways, unrelating themselves to
others who share social responsibility for the problem.

I take for granted that no reader will attribute to me the
belief that schools, even if they were to become exemplary by
my criteria, will be able to overcome the educational problems
of all children regardless of external factors that contribute to
their difficulties, for example, children of homeless families.
That schools can be more effective than they are with these
and all other children is a belief I hold. But it is grossly unfair
and unrealistic not to recognize that there are limits to what
we can expect schools to accomplish. This, among other things
I have noted, has not been squarely faced by educational reformers. Schools can be a vehicle for social change, but let us
not overestimate the strength, actual or potential, of that impact. Far more powerful is the impact of society on schools, an
impact that in recent decades has been as fruitless as it has
been powerful. There is a world of difference between viewing
schools as agents of socialization to the status quo and viewing
them as agents of social change. The status quo never calls for
its unhinging. A case can be made that our universities have
been to a degree agents of social change, a role frequently resented by many people. That that role has been possible is, in
part, a reflection of the vast difference in underlying values
and traditions between universities and public schools. When
the nature and consequences of that difference become a focus of discussion, reforming schools will take on a different
and challenging conceptual cast. Lest I be misunderstood: I

am not advocating that the aims of education should include changing society. But I do believe that if the particular aims I advocate are taken seriously, more minds would be liberated to think critically about school and society. The adjective *liberal* in liberal arts, historically at least, means liberation from narrowness and ignorance, and exposure to the best in human knowledge and accomplishment. To the extent that education is liberating—not only an acquisition of unconnected facts and skills or, worse yet, an anti-intellectual experience—the school-society relationship will not change, except to become more problematic for both.

To a significant degree, the major educational problems stem from the fact that educators not only accepted responsibility for schooling but, more fateful, also adopted a stance that essentially said: we know how to solve and manage the problems of schooling in America. Educators did not say: there is much that we do not know, many problems that are intractable to our efforts, and many individuals we are not reaching or helping. Put another way, educators were not calling attention to what was obvious to them in their daily work. Yes, they would say, we need more financial and other resources which, if made available, would improve education. That is why, when in the late fifties and early sixties the federal government began to provide additional resources, it seemed to educators as if they were in at the start of a new era in which they could really deliver on past promises. There were, needless to say, controversies about how to use the new resources, what should be changed and who should be changed. But no one was saying that those debates should be interpreted as indicating either that we were far from clear about what the problems were or that we had any solid ground for believing that any particular idea or practice would work as its proponents said. There were answers galore, a surfeit of promises, and it was understandable if the public gained the impression that the problems of schooling were like problems in mathematics in that they had clear answers. Matters were not helped any by educational critics and researchers, largely in our universities, who said not only that the emperor was naked but also that he was suffering from a terminal disease. They, with a few exceptions, did not say that the problems of schooling were long-standing and not amenable to quick remedies; that past emperors in the research community had misled them; that, actuarially speaking, most research being proposed would turn out to be, at best, fruitless and, at worst, harmful; that the research endeavor, however necessary, is no basis for devising timetables and communicating unjustified optimism; that the researcher, like the educational practitioner, wrestles with unknowns, trying to do his or her best with extraordinarily complex problems. Like the practitioners, the educational researchers promised the public more than they could deliver, implicitly suggesting a timetable that was wildly unrealistic. Far from seeing his kinship with the practitioner, the educational researcher tended to use the practitioner as scapegoat. And all the while, both researcher and practitioner knew in their hearts that they were seeking their ways through a forest of ignorance that seemed to grow trees faster than they could be cut down.

Let me make my point by analogy. Why is it that since the rise of scientific medicine in the latter half of the nineteenth century, we have not criticized and indicted the medical researcher and practitioner for not being able to cure the bulk of cancers—or, for that matter, hundreds of other bodily afflictions? Why has it not been said that medicine is either a failure or is quackery that does not deserve public support? One part of the answer is that the medical community has made a virtue of its ignorance insofar as its stance with the public is concerned. That community did not say that it would be able to cure cancers next year or twenty years from now. On the contrary, it emphasized the complexity and scope of the problem, the inadequacies of past and present conceptions and practices, the false starts and disappointments that await it and the public in the future, and the need for patience, forbearance, and the long-term view. In short, scientific medicine said: we will do our best, we will try to learn, but let us not underestimate the obstacles and conundrums we face.

This stance may not be the polar opposite of how the educational community has presented itself to the public, but it comes uncomfortably close. Why this has been and continues to be the case is beyond my present purpose, which is to emphasize that, to the extent that the educational community does not alter its stance, it is doomed. I am not suggesting that we compose a symphony of mea culpas in which the major theme is ignorance and the supporting chords are dysphoria and hopelessness. Nor am I suggesting that we change our stance only in order to obtain and increase the support of our various educational enterprises. The primary aim of this aspect of the challenge is two-fold: first, to get the educational community off the moral hook of promising more than it can deliver; and second, to increase public understanding of why the problems of schooling in our society are and will be so vexing. Implicit in this altered posture is a message: no longer will the educational community accept full responsibility for dealing with educational problems, most of which by their very nature are exacerbated by forces beyond the school. That is not to say, I should hasten to add, that educators will not deal with these problems as they manifest themselves in our schools, or that educators will not try to seek better approaches, but rather that these problems will be intractable as long as they are seen as the primary responsibility of educators. Just as the medical community does not accept responsibility for cancers caused by smoking, pollution, food additives, and scores of other possible carcinogens, the educational community cannot accept responsibility for problems originating in the larger society. Just as the medical community continues to deal clinically as best it can with etiological factors over which it has no control, so must the educational community do its best with problems beyond its control in the sense of prevention. Educators must assume leadership in relationship to diverse community groups and institutions, in a way that makes clear that responsibility is shared. As I have said elsewhere, for all practical purposes the answer to the question "Who owns the schools?" has been: educators. However understandable that was in terms of seeking professional status and of community compliance, it was a disastrous mistake, confusing leadership with shared responsibility.

I said earlier that these are dangerous times for education precisely because education is once again near the top of the national agenda. For one thing, the critics of education are again making scapegoats of educators as if the major problems are their responsibility and of their making. And proposals for change continue to assume that in the future this responsibility should remain where it is. I hear nothing from the educational community to challenge that assignment of responsibility. And therein is the danger that the proposed nostrums will be seen by the public, the ultimate victims, as answers. Who is saying that we are not dealing with problems that have solutions in the sense that four divided by two is two? Who is saying that however wondrous available technology (like the computer) may be, we are far from knowing how technology can or should be employed in a school, that it is not simply a matter of engineering technology into the classroom? (Is amnesia about the promise of teaching machines, the new math, the new biology, and the new physics total?) Who is saying that any effort at educational change, like the trials for a new drug, has to be concerned with side effects, indeed has to assume that there will be side effects so undesirable as to cause us to abort our efforts? Who is saying that we should never undertake any educational change or innovation unless there is a general recognition that we may fail outright or fall short of the mark, not because we lack confidence in what we will do but because we are realistic about the limitations of our knowledge, theoretical and practical, in an unpredictable world? The silence on these issues is, for all practical purposes, complete.

Let me illustrate my point with another analogy. The vast field of psychotherapy is incomprehensible apart from a grasp of the work and writings of Freud. It could be justifiably argued that, among the several lasting contributions he made, the most unassailable is his illumination of family dynamics. Freud did not use the word *system* as a concept to refer to the myriad of ways in which the behavior and personality of a family member condition and are conditioned by the behavior and personality of other family members. But to those who today read Freud, it will be obvious that he had a grasp, albeit an incomplete one, of the family as a social system in which understanding one part required understanding its transactional relationships to all other parts. Why, then, did he pursue a therapeutic approach that focused on a single part of the family system? Why was he unable to experiment with a therapy that directly addressed the family as a system? It is beyond my purposes to give a comprehensive answer to these questions, but surely an obvious part of the answer is that Freud the physician was embedded in a tradition in which one focused on the single individual. We know now that Freud and his epigones vastly overestimated the power of their therapy, a fact that toward the end of his life he seemed to accept. Indeed, the history of psychoanalysis, as theory and method, is one of changes in theory and practice in order to improve therapeutic outcomes—that is, to account for failures or a disappointing level of improvement. Today, the fruits of these earnest labors are not cause for gyrations of enthusiasm. And the same can be said for the literally scores of psychotherapies that are either offshoots of orthodox psychoanalysis or explicitly based on nonanalytic principles.[1]

Why did it take more than half a century after Freud's major contributions for family therapy to emerge? The reasons are several: disappointment with the outcomes of individual psychotherapy; the unacceptable length and cost of orthodox psychoanalysis or any of the prolonged psychotherapies; and, crucially, the recognition that a problem that arises within a system will be minimally ameliorated unless one deals with the system qua system. It is not by chance that family therapy emerged at the same time that theories of systems, human or otherwise, came to the fore in diverse fields. Nor is it fortuitous that central to the rationale for family therapy was the concept of power: how it is distributed, used, and interpreted by those who make up the system; how it determines, formally and informally, how the system reacts to threats to existing power relationships. Nor should it be surprising that family theory and therapy were not greeted enthusiastically by the psychotherapy establishment, and if that is less true today it is only somewhat less so. The fact is that, with a few exceptions in the university, family therapy developed outside of academic training centers.

There are several reasons for using family therapy for illustrative purposes in a discussion of school systems. The first reason is that comprehending a social system, large or small, requires a drastic alteration in the way one literally looks and acts in regard to the system: you are aware of parts, you do not ignore them, but your prime task is fathoming the processes and rules sustaining the system. That is not easy because, by our very nature, we see and respond to concrete, palpable objects, human or otherwise. We, so to speak, get drawn to parts. One cannot see a system; one has to conceptualize it. The second reason is that a systems orientation in no clear and direct way tells one when, where, or how to act to start the change process. Indeed, one's understanding of the system can change markedly as one takes steps to intervene. As any experienced family therapist will attest, one has to be prepared to change course, especially in the early phases. To initiate a change process according to a predetermined schedule of actions is self-defeating, as in the case of teachers who have lesson plans they slavishly follow, insensitive to how students are understanding, feeling, and responding.

The third reason was well put by a colleague: "Thinking in terms of a system, whether it is a family or school or school system, is intellectually demanding and messy; on the level of action it is like skating on thin ice or walking through a Mideast mine field, fearful that you miscalculated the dangers and regretful that you cannot go back to the starting point. Is it any wonder, then, that people concentrate on what they feel secure about doing even though they know that what they will do is an exercise in futility?" Unfortunately, in regard to educational reformers, my colleague is wrong in suggesting that they know better. Aside from a few reformers I shall discuss later, they do not. Thinking in terms of systems is not their cup of tea.

Proclaiming a systems approach is no badge of virtue or honor. Saying that you want to see things holistically is easy. But what does that mean for what you need to know? For the different starting points you should consider? For the kinds of resources you have and will require? For your time perspective? For the criteria by which you want your actions and outcomes to be judged? These questions require that I point out that anyone who seriously reads the family therapy literature will, I assume, arrive at two conclusions: there is by no means a clear consensus about the family as a social system, which in part explains the second conclusion that there is a bewildering array of therapeutic approaches to families, each presented as only a little short of perfection. At its conceptual core, family therapy is a major contribution to our thinking about system change. But at present there is very little compelling evidence that its wedding to practice has been consistent and efficacious. So, when I advocate a system approach to educational reform, it is not because I think we now have the understanding of school systems we need to have or that whatever understanding we have tells us clearly where our starting points might be. Far from it. What I do assert is that school systems have been intractable to the reforms sought by reformers. That sad, brute fact reflects acceptance of school systems as they are, focusing now on this part, now on that, this problem, that problem, as if the system in which they emerge is basically sound. A familiar joke is in order here. It is about the man who in the dead of winter was ill and went to his physician. After a thorough examination he was told to go home, take off all his clothes, open all the windows, stand in front of them, and breathe deeply and long. To which the man responded in amazement: "But, doctor, if I do that I will get pneumonia!" And the doctor replied: "*That* is something I know how to deal with." Educational reformers take note.

Finally, there is a fourth reason I used family therapy for illustrative purposes. Why, I asked earlier, did it take so long for this kind of therapy to emerge despite the fact that the dynamics of the family drama were described by Freud decades before? That kind of question has to be asked about our schools: what is there about school systems that prevents them from recognizing a problem before it reaches epidemic proportions? In other words, what is there about a school system that renders it virtually incapable of adopting a preventive stance? I offer the hypothesis that by organization, ideology, and knowledge, school personnel accept the responsibility to deal with the problems of *individuals*. They may not like it, they may feel adequate or inadequate, but they try to deal with the problems of individual children. They feel they have to (they cannot ignore a child who manifests a problem), especially if that child interferes with what in the school is normal routine. This may seem obvious, but precisely because it is so obvious— so right, natural, and proper—we too often fail to ask what the schools are doing to prevent these problems.

Let me illustrate this point by asking the reader to imagine that it is the late fifties or early sixties and you are the chief executive officer of General Motors, or Chrysler, or Ford. In that role you are given, at frequent intervals, a graph describing what percentage of the market you and your competition, foreign and domestic, have. In those early years you would have concluded that the share of the market held by foreign carmakers, especially German (Volkswagen) and Japanese, was nothing to worry about. If, from the vantage point of today, you examine those graphs for each successive year, it will be obvious that the line of the graph describing foreign market share was almost straight up—that is, the domestic market share was steadily decreasing. As we know, it is as if the domestic carmakers woke up to what was happening *after it had happened,* after their ability to compete had been weakened. The point here is not only that the domestic carmakers read the data wrong but also that they assumed that what was true in the past would be true in the future. They were governed by a set that simply did not permit them to ask: what might these graphs be saying and what actions might we take to fathom their meaning so as to take further actions calculated to be preventive, in contrast to those reflective of passivity and smugness? How does one determine whether one is dealing with a glitch or a trend? Although that question has no simple answer, it makes quite a difference if one approaches it with a clear preventive orientation rather than with one geared to problems that are so severe and pervasive that one is forced to take some remedial action, usually demonstrating that locking the barn door after the animals have fled solves nothing.

As in the case of Freud and family therapy, the infinite superiority of the preventive over the clinical stance is an old story. Why, then, is the clinical stance so much a feature of school systems and the preventive stance distinguished by its near total absence? As one superintendent of schools said to me: "Of course you are right. But who has time to think about preventing problems when we don't have enough time to deal with existing problems. Think preventively? Come off it. That is a luxury school systems cannot afford." That is a response I have gotten from scores of school personnel, and it is hard to be unsympathetic. I understand the response but I cannot excuse it—there comes a point when one has to pass judgment—because in other conversations with these same people (who are not few in number and whose roles in the system vary widely), I was told in unvarnished language that schools were dramatically better at identifying and categorizing problems than they were in dealing effectively with them. And I came to count on being told that the situation was getting worse, not better. No one ever saw anything contradictory in saying that the preventive stance was a luxury and that schools were relatively ineffective in stemming and dealing with the rising tide of difficult problems.[2]

I am far less judgmental of school personnel than I am of educational reformers who append their names to reports that are presented to the public as answers to major school problems. I expect that school personnel, whose phenomenology is so shaped by their socialization and embeddedness in a problem-creating, problem-focused system, will have difficulty adopting a stance that would permit them to understand the nature of the system in its complexity. I expect more, however, from those outside the educational arena who accept the responsibility for recommending change. I had hoped that these reformers would have less difficulty.

One last argument by analogy. Over the past half-century, with cyclical regularity, medical educators have noted and bemoaned the fact that physicians, generally speaking, lacked an appropriate degree of caring and compassion. That is to say, they approached patients in intimidating and insensitive ways that not only caused discomfort but unduly restricted the range of information they obtained, thus missing opportunities to be helpful both clinically and preventively. Each of these reports, all of which had the imprimatur of distinguished medical educators, criticizes the nature and ambience of medical training and recommends curriculum changes. And each report concludes that the situation not only has not improved but has gotten worse. How does one explain these failures of medical education reform? The reports are thunderingly silent about the question even though they make clear that there is something about the culture of medical schools that is lethal to the intended changes. But when you read their recommendations, from which the history of past efforts is totally absent, they are strikingly similar to those in past reports. They do not pursue what is clear (on and between the lines) in their reports: the system of medical education—its underlying axioms, traditions, selection criteria, incentives, and distribution of power—will overwhelm any non-system-oriented reform. The reader who thinks that it is only in our public schools that educational reform has failed should read my book *Caring and Compassion in Clinical Practice* (1985). In that book I examine efforts to improve caring and compassion in medicine, psychiatry, clinical psychology, and teaching, and among lawyers in family practice.

I have emphasized that adopting a system stance is no easy matter and, given our state of knowledge and experience, it does not now provide us with a course for action. But of one thing I am certain: any effort at reform has to have as its goal a change in existing power relationships in the system. That, I hasten to add, is no guarantee of success but it is a precondition for other alterations in the system. That point has received increased recognition in recent years, albeit in a somewhat murky and narrow way. In the next chapter I examine the nature of that recognition, the opportunities it suggests, the dilemmas that arise, and the predictable conflicts that put a premium on courage and vision. Changing a system is not for the conceptually and interpersonally fainthearted.

## Notes

1. I do not want to be interpreted as damning psychotherapeutic practice. I have no doubt whatsoever that some people have benefited from psychotherapy and that some psychotherapists obtain far better results than others. Why this is so is very far from clear. From my experience, observations, and reading, I conclude (cautiously) that where individual psychotherapy has had some degree of success it has been because the individual's role in the family system has been a focus. What my comments are intended to convey is the conclusion that, generally speaking, the modest effects of individual psychotherapy, as well as its outright failures, are in large measure attributable to working with a part and not a part in a system.

2. David Kearns, chairman of the Xerox Corporation, is one of the most committed people to improving our schools. I do not know him. It is clear from what he has said and written that he has concluded that unless that improvement takes place we will become a second-rate society, educationally and economically. Indeed, he has a six-point plan "to radically change the public education system in the United States." Restructuring, choice, professionalism, standards, values, federal responsibility: these are headings indicative of Mr. Kearns's plan (*New York Times*, December 17, 1989). As I hope will become clear in later chapters, what Mr. Kearns regards as radical is quite conventional. When he compares education in the United States and Japan—and guess who comes up smelling like a rose—he betrays his superficial understanding of both our culture and our schools. With friends like Mr. Kearns, the opponents of educational change need not fear for the status quo. He is regarded as an "enlightened" businessman, as he certainly is compared to others in comparable positions. But he certainly does not understand schools the way he does Xerox.

# 4

## ALTERING POWER
## RELATIONSHIPS

IN MY DICTIONARY THE FIRST OF SEVERAL DEFINITIONS OF POWER is "possession of control, or authority, or influence over others." Another, more muted, definition given is "the ability to act or produce an effect." The first definition emphasizes a feature of interpersonal relationships, which explains why in that context the exercise of power is so frequently accompanied by conflict. To have power "over" someone is an invitation to conflict. The second definition is less stark in that it does not contain the idea of one person being able to compel another to do something. It is the first definition that is appropriate to the aims of unions seeking to restrict the range and substance of actions of those with legal authority for the school system. It is an openly adversarial relationship in which power suffuses the thinking of all participants and is most clearly demonstrated by strike action. No one is in doubt that power is the name of the game. Indeed, it was not until the rise of militant teacher unions that the public generally became aware of how power was allocated and used in school systems—but not only within the system. The rise of those unions exploded the myth that ultimate authority for educational policy resided exclusively in boards of education. There was the mayor's office (and the state legislature) that had to be taken into account in any settlement between the unions and the board of education.

Too many people today have forgotten or are unaware of the fact that before the unions gained strength the teacher was in a most unequal power relationship with the policymakers. It is not hyperbole to say that teachers almost totally lacked power either in terms of "control over" anyone or "the ability to act or produce an effect." Understanding that powerlessness is important for several reasons. First, it illuminates why, then and now, many people have not regarded teachers as professionals—that is, because they have little or no control over the rendering of their services. They are paid help doing what they have been told to do. Second, it explains why it took so long, together with altered social changes, for teachers to overcome their resistance to unionization. To become part of the *labor* movement was tantamount to confirming the view that teachers were not professionals. Third, it also explains why, in their initial displays of strength, teacher unions focused not on professional or educational issues but on "bread and butter" ones. Their challenges to existing power relationships steered clear of what is ordinarily meant by matters of educational policy and practice. A fourth reason is that the unions justified their existence and militancy on the grounds of fairness of remuneration and improvement in educational outcomes. Not only were teacher salaries scandalously low but if they were raised, it was argued, it would increase morale and act as a magnet to attract the ablest people into teaching. Implicitly, the unions accepted the assessment that there were many things wrong with our schools, not the least of which was the lack of status and respect accorded teachers by the educational policymakers and administrators.

There is one other reason for recalling this recent history as a means for understanding what is happening today. That is the recognition, on the part of unions and the public generally, that despite the economic successes of the unions and despite the vast sums of money poured into our school systems in the past twenty-five years, educational outcomes did not discernibly improve. Whatever power realignments the unions brought about did not change educational outcomes. In light of that disappointment (which I predicted), the problem was reformulated: what was there about the culture of the school and school systems that was inimical to desired outcomes? Granted that in terms of importance and fairness teachers deserved increased remuneration, and granted that school systems had more problems than money, should we not look elsewhere than to economics for an explanation for why it appears that the more things change the more they remain the same? And to that question, the most frequently articulated answer revolved around the processes of decision making in matters educational. More specifically, the problem was one of a bureaucratic tradition and style in which those directly or indirectly affected by an educational policy did not have a voice in formulating that policy. The definition of power as "the ability to act or produce an effect" was one that in practice applied only to a small number of school personnel and that did not include teachers. The reformulation clearly suggested that the educational decision-making process ignored the creativity and experience of people with an obvious stake in improving our schools. If that process became more open and inclusive, the substance and direction of policies would take on more boldness, experimentation, and vision, which would engender a degree of commitment that the participants are now unable or unwilling to give. New participants, new ideas, a greater willingness to depart from stifling tradition would be the fruits of new power alignments.

No one more than Albert Shanker, president of the American Federation of Teachers, articulated this formulation, and long before today when that formulation is gaining adherents. Anyone following his column in the Sunday *New York Times* from its inception in 1970 to today would be impressed by a number of points. First, and perhaps most remarkable, Shanker, unlike most people in the educational arena, is capable of owning up to his past parochialism. Put more positively and correctly, he has been able to enlarge his understanding of what is at stake and needs to be done. Second, without in any way downgrading the significance of economic factors, he came to see that no less important were the ways in which stifling tradition and a feudal style of organization suppressed changes and innovation. Indeed, he even raised the question of whether his organization, for the sake of saving our public schools, could or should restrict itself only to the economic betterment of its constituents. Could it afford to stay within the bread-and-butter traditions of the labor movement? Third, teachers have to be part of the educational decision-making process not only as recognition of or incentive to professional status but also because the daily lives of teachers are influenced by decisions in which they have no voice. Teachers have something to contribute but they have no forum. Fourth, and truly astounding, if teachers were given an enlarged role in policy formulation *and* implementation, the educational changes to which they would commit themselves should not be obstructed by provisions of existing contracts. Fifth, although his obvious main concern is about the role of teachers in decision making and, therefore, accountability, Shanker is clear that other groups in the community have to have a role in deciding what schools do and are about. Sixth, he has been enthusiastically supportive of those few school systems (such as those in Pittsburgh, Rochester, and Miami) that are exceptions to my earlier generalization about the absence of instances of system-mandated changes in teacher participation in the formulation and implementation of educational policy.

In later pages of this chapter, as well as in the next chapter, I shall call into question the assumption that opening up the decision-making process will necessarily improve educational outcomes. That I am in favor of opening up that process goes without saying, but I do not justify it because I think that changing power relationships will improve educational outcomes. Changing such relationships is a necessary but not sufficient basis for desirable outcomes. As Shanker knows well from his earlier battles in New York about community participation and decentralization, altering power relationships can alter power relationships but nothing else. Shanker deserves a great deal of credit for a level of intellectual and moral leadership all too rare in education. Compared to William Bennett, a former Secretary of Education, Shanker is an educational statesman par excellence.

Power realignments in the educational arena have always been a feature of the history of our public schools, but it was only in the post-World War II era that the question of "Who owns the schools?" began to be raised. That question was not being asked in a legal, legislative, or constitutional framework; in that framework the answer was relatively clear, albeit unrevealing. In reality, several questions were being raised. On a state and local level, who were the people involved—directly or indirectly, formally or informally—in formulating overall educational policies? How and by whom were these policies disseminated and implemented throughout a school system, and with what translations and transformations? How well did teachers comprehend and implement these policies and with what degree of uniformity? These questions were not answerable by looking at laws, stated policies, or job descriptions. They were questions about who in real life participates in what ways and for what purposes and with what effects in educational decision making. And they were being asked for two related reasons: dissatisfaction with educational outcomes, and challenges (especially in the sixties) to every major social institution in the society. Undergirding all of these questions was a moral-political one: who *should* participate in educational decision making? And the general answer was: any individual or group who directly or indirectly would be affected by a decision should stand in some relationship to the decision-making process. That answer began to inform decision making in various social arenas, such as the environment, highway construction, and housing complexes. It would have been surprising if that answer had not spurred different groups to try to alter the traditional style of educational decision making in our schools. That educators generally were made more sensitive to the implications of that answer goes without saying, but it did not go much beyond sensitivity. Rhetoric and even intentions changed, but power relationships remained much as they were.

There were two instructive exceptions. The first was the rise in strength and militancy of teacher unions. What was fascinating here was that boards of education zealously enjoined the participants in collective bargaining from any matter involving educational decision making. Collective bargaining had to do with bread-and-butter issues, working conditions, a stance quite in keeping with the traditions of unions in this country. The union did not challenge boards in regard to educational policy. The fact is, as both sides came quickly to realize, that any agreement about money and working conditions has to influence, directly or indirectly, to small or large degree, the substance, scope, and style of educational decision making. Anyone who doubts this glimpse of the obvious has never sat in on meetings of boards of education or of superintendents and their staffs. What will the union say? How will it react? Those are the kinds of questions that get raised in discussions of any important proposal for educational change. But the greatest significance of the rise of the strong teacher unions lies less in this glimpse of the obvious than in the historical fact that those above the level of teachers who were responsible for educational decision making fought bitterly against the recognition of these unions. And among those who fought most strenuously were individuals who envisioned a future in which bread-and-butter agendas would surely have added to them what they regarded as the most evil consequence of all: *educational* policy issues. It is possible to write the history of American education from a number of perspectives, but one of the most illuminating would detail how decision makers sought to restrict the kinds of individuals and groups who would participate in decision making.

The second exception was Public Law 94–142 of 1975, the so-called "mainstreaming" legislation for handicapped children (the word "mainstreaming" does not appear in that legislation), to which I have already referred. It was an act intended to transform educational policy and practice in the nation's schools. Generally speaking, educators were not among the ardent advocates of the legislation, and among the several reasons for this lack of enthusiasm were features of the law that would alter customary power relationships in schools. For example,

one of those features in this complex law spelled out in unusual detail the rights of parents to participate in decision making about their children. Indeed, one of the people who helped
to draft that legislation told me (paraphrased): "The real guts
of that legislation is in its civil rights features. We wanted to
ensure that parents would participate in, and in certain respects, have veto power over decisions affecting them and their
children. The day is past when school personnel, with the support of boards of education, make decisions and *then* inform
parents." It is significant that this feature of the law is today
honored more in the breach than in the practice. The important point is that, as in the case of their response to unionization of teachers, the decision makers wanted no change in who
participated in or would affect educational decision making.
Those who wield power do not look kindly on any possible
dilution of that power. I do not say this critically but rather as
a statement of empirical fact. To gloss over that fact is to reduce mightily the chances that any significant proposal to alter
power relationships will be successful, even in part.

The above is by way of prologue to discussion of a proposal
contained in the 1988 Carnegie report that teachers should
formally participate in educational decision making. That report, especially the proposal about teachers and decision making, received a good deal of attention in the mass media. In
our major newspapers there were editorials endorsing the proposal, usually on the grounds that if teachers were indeed professionals, as they should be, they should have a voice in the
formulation of educational policy. If teaching as a profession
was to attract the quality of students commensurate with the
importance of the role of teacher, we should no longer exclude
teachers from the decision-making process. To continue to exclude them was a manifestation of the too widely held view that
teachers were incapable of responsibly participating in the process. Predictably, organizations representing school administrators were critical of the proposal. The Secretary of Education
made it clear that he regarded the proposal as misguided, ill
advised, and divisive.

I had two reactions to the proposal. The first was gratitude that the proposal and its justification had been incisively formulated. This was not the first time that the proposal had been advanced, but heretofore it had been advocated only by representatives of teachers. The second reaction was disappointment about several omissions: to identify the nature and sources of opposition, to identify the predictable problems that implementation would engender, to be specific regarding when and about what teachers should be involved and the implications of the proposals for the preparation of teachers and administrators. I assume that the groups responsible for the report knew quite well that the proposal would arouse controversy and that the greater the detail in which it was embedded the more likely that attention would be diverted from the main message: teachers should in some way be part of educational decision making.

I am aware that there are schools in which teachers participate in decision making in regard to the classroom and the school generally. With very few exceptions, teacher participation was not a consequence of a system-wide policy proclaimed by the superintendent or the board of education. It was a consequence of a school policy initiated and supported by the principal. How would one explain these instances? Is each instance a reflection of idiosyncratic factors from which no generalization is possible? Was the initiative or support from the principal in any way related to the formal preparation of the principal—that is, to the curriculum or credentialing process he or she had experienced? Or were they a reflection of deeply held beliefs about the uses and abuses of asymmetrically distributed power? In each of these instances, by what criteria of "success" did the participants want to be judged: a sustained sense of professional collegiality, professional growth, student achievement scores? Why are these instances so few in number? I raise these questions because the proposal for teacher participation should be judged by, among other things, more than anecdotal evidence. It is a proposal of such significance for the public interest that it requires us to go beyond expressions of personal opinion. To the extent that critics of and advocates for the proposal are content to base their arguments on whether they think it is "a good or bad idea," we will be witness again—an old story in the educational arena—to a debate in which rhetoric and name-calling will effectively rule out the attainment of clarity about what is at stake and the universe of alternatives the proposal should engender in regard to implementation. So, for example, it is understandable if advocates for the proposal point to instances in which the desired effects seem to have been achieved. But these advocates have to recognize that these instances (in my experience) share the characteristic of being voluntary—that is, they were not consequences of a policy directive from on high. They were not instances of an explicit central office policy that mandated teacher participation. (There are a few exceptions I shall note later.) Were the writers of the Carnegie report suggesting that teacher participation should be "encouraged" or "mandated"? Obviously, they would not argue against encouragement, but many of them must have known that encouragement alone would have no dramatic effect on the frequency with which teachers would participate in educational decision making. If the intention was that the proposal be institutionalized, we cannot ignore what we have learned from the long history of efforts to introduce a significant change in the culture of the school. It is not a history conducive to optimism.

In the past several years I have met with many groups of teachers. None of these occasions was organized to discuss teacher participation in decision making, but I always knew that at some point in the discussion teacher dissatisfaction with their status would come up. I took advantage of these opportunities to ask the following question: "Imagine the situation that, beginning next September, teachers would be accorded a role in educational decision making, and you are being asked to discuss what that role should be. What would you recommend?" The question was unfair in the sense that these teachers had not come prepared to discuss it. It was not unfair because almost all of the teachers had made it plain that they felt they had no voice in regard to matters affecting them in their role, and they wanted a voice.

The first response to my question was a kind of bewildered

silence. That response was noteworthy because it revealed that although they very strongly accepted teacher participation as a matter of principle, they had not confronted the implications of that principle for practice or implementation. I usually broke the silence by saying that I was no better off than they were in answering my own question. Unlike me, they would have to live with whatever recommendations they would make, and I was sincerely interested in their response. No one disputed my next statement that I found it incomprehensible that at no time in their formal preparation for teaching had they been exposed to the issues surrounding the status of teachers in educational decision making.

I could count on being asked several questions, which went something like this: "Your question is not clear. Educational decisions, some important some not, are being made all of the time. Some of them affect me very directly both personally and professionally. Others affect me indirectly but significantly. For example, some educational decisions—like those concerning curriculum, the form and substance of report cards, criteria for promotion, size of class, and choice of a superintendent— affect every teacher in every school. Are you asking how we think we should be related to decisions intended to affect everyone in the system, teachers and students? But then there are decisions that will affect only me and my school—choosing a principal, hiring new teachers, how I am evaluated, the composition of the students I am given, and allocation of materials. If as teachers we feel we should participate in all of these kinds of decisions, how could we organize ourselves to be represented and where would we get the time to participate? And what do you mean by participate? Would our role be advisory or voting?"

It did not take long for the teachers to come to several conclusions. The first was that the proposal for teacher participation was far more complex in its implication for action than they had imagined. The second was that it would be a mistake at this time for teachers to seek to participate in all important educational decisions. And the third was that teachers should begin by participating in those decisions that peculiarly and

powerfully affect them on a daily basis in their own schools.
Once the teachers began to think about their real selves in their
individual schools, their bewilderment and confusion disap-
peared and, in almost every one of these groups, they stopped
directing questions to me and began to discuss among themselves, clearly and forthrightly, the educational decisions to which
they wanted to be related in a meaningful way. There was an
amazing degree of unanimity about two related types of decisions. Indeed, once these two types of decisions were identified, there seemed to be a collective sigh of relief and satisfaction because they had come to answers that truly spoke to their
needs for professional recognition. They did not want to discuss the matter further and so we returned to our original
agenda.

The first area of decision making in which teachers wanted
a significant role was in the selection of new teachers for open-
ings in their schools. The second was in the selection of a new
principal. The reasons can be summarized in this paraphrase:
"Each school has its own character and atmosphere. Each school
is like a family, and families vary tremendously in their history
and in the ties that bind. And like all families, it has its assets
and deficits. When you bring in a new teacher or a principal,
you are bringing in someone who will affect our lives, positively or negatively, for what can be a long time. As teachers
we want a role in shaping our family's destiny. Is it unreason-
able to ask for this in a matter that can significantly alter our
lives?"

It is worth noting that at no point in these discussions was
there an attempt to define the role of teachers in these decisions. No one challenged the authority of administrators to make
final decisions. No one suggested a "procedure" to which
teachers would be formally related. They were not advocating
an informal role. They were advocating a role by which teacher
representation and opinion would be for the record, ensuring
that whoever was responsible for final decisions would know
what teacher opinion was.

Significant to me in these discussions was the implicit assumption that the question I had posed involved an exercise

of the imagination which, however interesting, would forever remain in the realm of fantasy. As teachers they had no responsibility for matters that they believed affected the educational enterprise—that is, to the extent that teachers had no voice in these matters, they shouldered no responsibility for the negative consequences that their impotence produced. At the same time that they accepted responsibility for what happened in their classrooms, discharging that responsibility was negatively affected by their powerlessness in educational decision making.

It is both ironic and fitting that teacher participation in decision making should have come to the fore in the bicentennial of the American Constitution, because the 1787 Constitutional Convention struggled with three major issues: rights, representation, and distribution of power. If the participants were poignantly aware of anything, it was the abuse over the centuries of unilateral, centralized sources of power. How can power be distributed and checked so that the voice of the people can be both represented and heeded? How can the forums of governance be structured to be sensitive to the needs and rights of the citizenry? The proposal for teacher participation in decision making clearly challenges the rationale for governance of our schools. The challenge is coming not only from teachers but also from a myriad of groups angered and puzzled by the fruitlessness of efforts to improve our schools. There are those who would not be unhappy to see the dismantling of our school systems. There are those, in and out of the system, who have given up trying to effect change, and there are many more who continue to try but who basically accept—certainly they do not tamper with—the existing governance structure.

What characterizes the attempts of these different groups is their inability or unwillingness to confront the issues faced by the Founding Fathers: rights, representation, and power. For a short while in the turbulent sixties these issues did get raised—for example, community-parent participation in decision making, the rights of students, and the like. But this occurred in such an adversarial context that the general import of the issues was glossed over or simply not explored. In the sixties many people accepted the principle that those who, directly or indirectly, would be affected by a public policy should stand in some relationship to the decision-making process from which a policy emerges. What did acceptance of that principle mean for governance of our school systems? If that question had been systematically explored, it would have been immediately obvious that it had import for groups other than teachers, parents, and students. Anyone familiar with our school systems, especially urban ones, well knows that principals and other administrators feel that they are too frequently unrelated to decision making that significantly affects them and those for whom they are responsible. In this respect they are as much victims as are the teachers. One of my criticisms of the Carnegie proposal for teacher participation in school governance is that it creates the mistaken impression that all those above the level of teacher are meaningfully related to the policy- and decision-making process. If administrators have taken a very dim view of the Carnegie proposal, it is in part because they see it as but another instance of dilution of their weak sense of relatedness to significant decision making. As one principal said to me: "I have next to no role now in educational decision making that affects me and my school. Why should I feel enthusiastic about the Carnegie proposal?" The fact is that a large majority of school personnel feel that they have no meaningful role in decision making.

Two things are obvious from what I have said thus far. The first is that I accept the principle of participation in decision making. My acceptance is based on the belief that when a process makes people feel that they have a voice in matters that affect them, they will have a greater commitment to the overall enterprise and will take greater responsibility for what happens to the enterprise. Second, the absence of such a process ensures that no one feels responsible, that blame will always be directed externally, that adversarialism will be a notable feature of school life.

At the present time, and at best, each teacher feels responsibility only for what happens in his or her classroom, the degree of responsibility varying with the degree to which the teacher feels that school and system policies do not negatively impact on that classroom. The teacher feels far less responsibility for the school as a social-educational setting than for his or her classroom. What would require explanation is if teachers felt otherwise. Why should they feel responsibility for the school qua school when they have had no role in determining who should be teaching there, who the principal should be, and what the agenda for collegial discussion should be? I am reminded here of a book I wrote with others in 1966, *Psychology in Community Settings*. One chapter in that book elicited more spontaneous response from teachers than anything else in that large volume. It was written by Murray Levine and the chapter title was "Teaching is a Lonely Profession." Levine made clear in that chapter that teachers poignantly feel socially and intellectually isolated in their encapsulated classrooms, the polar opposite of the sense of community—that is, the sense of belonging and mutuality.[1]

Any advocate for teacher participation in decision making has to be extraordinarily clear about the consequences they envision if the proposal is implemented. More specifically, it would be egregiously wrong to justify the proposal on the grounds that it will improve educational scores, decrease dropout rates, and transform uninteresting classrooms into interesting ones. It is understandable if one hopes that such consequences will take place, but there is nothing in the substance of the proposal that justifies the conclusion that altering the participants in the decision-making process (that is, changing the forces of power) will improve the quality, innovativeness, or creativity of educational decisions. But even for those in whom hope springs eternal, the question they must confront is, how long will it take for the desired outcomes to be discernible? Assume for the moment that through the forces of inscrutable magic, beginning tomorrow, teachers will have a meaningful role in decision making. When should we expect that this momentous change will impact on educational outcomes in ways that everyone desires? In the "Our Towns" column of the *New York Times* for January 1, 1988, there appeared the following:

In one of the more exciting social experiments of the year, Rochester decided to pay as if urban teaching were an important job—up to $70,000 a year. But already there is uneasiness. Adam Urbanski, union president, says where he goes, people say: "It's four months. Has the dropout rate gone down yet?" He says there is resistance from a quarter of the principals, who feel that increased teacher power is decreased principal power.

Time perspective and institutional change—how clearly and realistically we integrate these two concepts will be fateful for how we justify any proposal for educational change. If we have learned anything in recent decades, it is that changing mission statement, curricula, procedures, or laws in no way guarantees desired outcomes. And that will be no less true in the case of teacher participation in decision making. The justification for teacher participation is political-moral in that it rests on the value that those who are vitally affected by decisions should stand in some meaningful relation to the decision-making process. As I must emphasize again, that does not necessarily mean that altering the process will make for better decisions. What it does mean is that in implementing the proposal, we are starting a process of change long overdue, the consequences of which are uncertain in the short and long term. Nothing will be more subversive of the process than an unhistorical, unrealistic conception of the relationship between time perspective and institutional change.

I have already indicated that in the case of teachers their power status is, with a few exceptions, no different than heretofore. There is no clamoring among policymakers, or the public generally, to foster such a change. It is grossly premature to say that it is an idea whose time has come. That should be warning enough to those who underestimate the obstacles to change where power is buttressed by long-standing tradition and self-interest. And it also should serve as a caution to those insensitive to the fact that giving new power to those unaccustomed to having power presents new problems. I am reminded here of the effort of the superintendent of schools of a large city, together with the head of the teacher union, to give the faculty of several high schools the power to make whatever changes they thought necessary to improve their schools. The one restriction was that they had to stay within existing budgets. There was abundant evidence that in each of these high schools there were many problems teachers and principals would have liked to correct, and potentially could correct, that did not require new money. Representatives from these high schools were asked to meet ten times over a period of a few months in a nonurban retreat site conducive to thought, reflection, and discussion. The enthusiasm in the first few meetings was high, but by the fifth or sixth meeting it plummeted. When the superintendent and head of the teacher union became aware of this and inquired about its causes, they were told by the group: "Too many of us simply don't believe that we really will be allowed to do what we want to do, and that after we spend all of this time coming up with our plans, we will be told that this or that is not possible, or practical, or supportable." This anecdote was related to me by the head of the teacher union, who said (paraphrased): "I really did not comprehend the depths of the distrust that teachers have about the intentions of administrators. Everything in their experience taught them two things: don't believe the sincerity of what you are told, and don't allow yourself to hope that a real change is possible because you will be disappointed. But there was another factor at work, and that is that if they exercised the new power we were giving them and things did not work out well, they would be clobbered. They truly feared exercising the new power we had given them. The closer they came to realizing what they wanted to do, the changes and conflicts they would face, the less enamored they were with their new power." Changing power relationships consistent with the goals of the changes is, to indulge understatement, no simple affair. History, tradition, overlearned attitudes, and unrealistic time perspectives ensure turmoil.

From the standpoint of a system orientation, altering the

power status of teachers addresses only one of the features of loci of power. For example, and related to the anecdote above, what about the power relationships between school systems and universities that educate and train teachers and school administrators? It never fails to surprise me that in the plethora of reports on improving schools, that question is rarely raised and then only in the most superficial way, leading one to believe that those relationships are nonproblematic. This is in large part because these relationships are subtle, informal, and indirect.

From the standpoint of the school system, the power of the university resides in its legally sanctioned role in preparing, certifying, or credentialing school personnel. School systems depend on these programs for their personnel needs but they have little or no power to influence them. They, so to speak, have to take what is given them. They see university faculty as having a more elevated status and, publicly at least, they accord them respect for superior knowledge and understanding of the educational process and its problems. They do not challenge them, if only because it may constrict the personnel pool, qualitatively and quantitatively, that these programs make available to them. In the educational hierarchy, university faculty are at the top. And, it must be emphasized, these programs are crucial to school personnel seeking to fulfill continuing education requirements or to move up in the hierarchy.

From the standpoint of the university, the school systems hold power in three ways. First, they provide field sites for pre-professional experience. Second, they are a source of students for a variety of programs, old and new, without whom these programs and their faculties could not be justified financially. And third, they serve as sites for research by university faculty who, without such sites, could not carry out their investigative projects, write them up, publish them, and use them for academic upward mobility. The university needs the school system and its personnel, and that need mightily dilutes the expression of criticism of the schools by university faculty. Usually, what these university faculty will express privately is far more polemical than what they will say publicly. University faculty generally consider themselves superior to school personnel in terms of understanding issues, problems, and courses of action, and in intellectual leadership. It is a stance of superiority that they, wittingly or unwittingly, communicate quite effectively to school personnel, who do nothing to dispute it because they cannot afford to. It is a stance fed by a disdain for the performance of school personnel.

The symbiotic relationship between schools and the university is marked by strong ambivalence. School personnel often derogate the quality and relevance of their professional education, and university faculty look upon the poor quality of our schools as in large measure due to the poor intellectual and personal qualities of school personnel. The expression of this ambivalence is kept in check by the power of each to affect the other adversely. As a consequence, rather than depart from convention, these programs change by addition—that is, they do more of what they have done before and in the same way.[2]

In light of what I have described about the recognition given in the past decade to altering the power status of teachers, one would think that the issues would have received serious discussion in the preparation of teachers and administrators. After all, like it or not, these issues go for the jugular in the existing pattern of relationships. If these issues have hardly affected practice, they still deserve the most serious scrutiny and discussion. If comprehensive, no-holds-barred discussions do not take place in these university programs, why should one expect them to take place anywhere else? Should not these programs prepare teachers and administrators, to some degree at least, to begin to think about these issues—their ethical-moral-political implications, the attitudes one has to adopt, the attitudes one has to unlearn, the predictable turmoil, sensitivity to intended and unintended consequences, and the assumption that changes in power relationships will positively affect educational outcomes? I am here not advocating discussion about a world that does not exist, about pie-in-the-sky ideas, but about issues that are surfacing from a general dissatisfaction with public schools. And I am not advocating discussion pro or con but from the point of view that the issues have a long history and are not simple issues, that they are gaining more currency and adherents, that those entering teaching and administration cannot afford to be ignorant about what is at stake, and that the wave of the future may not be far from land. Can one advocate changing the power status of teachers and administrators and ignore the existing power relationships between schools and university programs that prepare teachers and administrators? Apparently so, when one focuses on one kind of change in power alignments and ignores other relevant power relationships—that is, when one does not understand schools as social systems in their relationship to other systems.

If the instances in which significant changes in the power status of teachers have been (are being) attempted are few in number, that is not the case in regard to an altered status of parents and others in educational decision making. Several states have already mandated that in each school there will be a council or advisory group that is to have a say in what a school plans and does. This, of course, did not come about because school systems wanted such legislation. As one superintendent of schools in one of these states said to me: "We wanted that legislation the way we wanted a hole in the head." That was not said by a superintendent satisfied with existing practice or in principle opposed to opening up the decision-making process to new groups. He went on to explain: "We—by which I mean principals, other administrators, teachers, and *me*—are simply not prepared to deal with the implications and consequences of the legislation. And by not being prepared, I mean in terms of time and attitude. When I think of all the problems we are now dealing with, by no means well, and that we now will have to deal with new groups and procedures, I confess to feeling fearful, inadequate, overwhelmed. If you were to ask me right now how we will go about all this, I would have to say my mind is a blank. But that is only half of the picture. How prepared are these new groups to have a meaningful input? I am not putting them down when I say that they are less prepared than we are. As I said to you earlier, I believe in an expansion of participants in formulating policy and having a role in the nitty-gritty of decision making. What sends me up a wall are two things: it will all turn out to be a charade, all appearance and no substance, and my feeling that those responsible for the legislation are expecting that in one or two years test scores will go up, school dropouts will go way down, and peace will reign. You will excuse me if I am not optimistic."

I do not relate this anecdote to suggest that I am opposed to such legislation.[3] In this very real world one cannot count on time to correct what needs to be corrected. (Desegregation in this country and apartheid in South Africa are examples of what I mean.) In societies and their institutions changes in power between and among groups have their predictable problems, conflicts, and costs. What concerns me is that, in the educational arena, those who advocate such changes, especially mandated changes, are either ignorant of the predictable problems or so unsophisticated about the dynamics of institutional change that they end up with timetables and expectations that are so unrealistic that one can safely predict that they will end up blaming the victims. It is easy to mandate the initiation of a process of change. It is not easy—and for some it is apparently impossible—to initiate that process from the standpoint of several questions: What are the predictable problems? How embedded are they in the history, tradition, and organization of school systems? What courses of preventive action might be employed, at least to minimize these problems? When and why should we expect which outcomes?

I am not at this point addressing the management of the change process—that is, I am not talking about technical matters. Prior to such matters, and crucially influential to them, is a comprehensive understanding of the system in its complexity, dynamics, traditions, and relationships to other systems. As will be discussed in a later chapter, such understanding cannot, should not, be informed by the customary superficial answers to the questions: What are the near- and long-term aims of education? And for whom? The customary answer is that schools are for the personal, moral, civic, and intellectual development of children. That seemingly self-evident answer is where the problem originates. That is like saying that parents exist only for the welfare of their children. As any semicandid parent will attest, their existence is far more complicated than such an answer suggests.

It would indeed be surprising if what I have said in this chapter about schools (problems and perspectives) was relevant only to them—that is, that their history and current problems are truly unique and that their inadequacies, and the public's dissatisfaction with their performance, bear little or no similarity to what happens to other sectors of the society. That is not the case, and I refer specifically to the industrial sector. Today we are used to hearing about the shortcomings, shortsightedness, and self-defeating practices of this sector. Whereas this sector once was Hertz to lesser Avises, it is now struggling to be competitive, and not doing all that well. The criticisms and explanations have been many:

1.  Those in management (kin to educational policymakers and administrators) have focused on the here and now or very near future in that their aim is to maximize profits now. (That is like riveting on achievement tests as the single most important criterion of success.)
2.  Those who run these industrial organizations ignored changes in what was happening in other parts of the world, as if they were immune to the consequences of those changes. (That is like saying that school systems were insensitive to what was happening in their communities.)
3.  Business schools in our universities prepared their students not for a changing world but for one that assumed the future would be a carbon copy of the past. They also accepted and inculcated organizational values that essentially reinforced adversarial relationships and glossed over the obligations of companies to further not only increased competence of their employees but, crucially, also the personal commitment of these employees to the enterprise. (That is like saying that school systems will not improve as long as they ignore the needs of various groups of school personnel.)
4.  If whatever we mean by the work ethic has deteriorated,

it in part derives from a neglect of the centrality of human values in the workplace. If there was a time when that neglect had no adverse consequences for profitability, that time is past, but business leaders seem unwilling or unable to adapt to these altered attitudes. (That is like saying that educators do not know how to face up to the fact that what they are doing is simply not working.)

5. Large businesses (like large school systems) have layers of bureaucracy that guarantee that the owners or planners or policymakers are isolated from most of their employees and their needs, complaints, advice, and so on.

6. After World War II, when the preeminence and economic strength of the country were facts, and profits seemed assured regardless of quality of product, American business felt little need to ask: who are our customers or stakeholders, what obligations do we have to them, how do we give them a stake in what we do? It was not a public-be-damned attitude but a we-don't-have-to-worry stance—that is, they will buy what we give them. (That is like educators who assumed that what they were doing would continue to be accepted by communities.)

7. The tendency of business today to look to the federal government for help in becoming more competitive and profitable—by means of quotas on foreign imports and tax incentives—diverts attention from changes that industry could and should make independent of government. Money is not the primary problem. The primary problem is how one can change not tax incentives, but existing personal incentives so that they will give all in the organization a greater sense of competence and commitment, i.e., changing existing power relationships. If we do not deal more creatively with a self-destructive adversarialism, the consequences are incalculable.

There are more criticisms and explanations but the foregoing should be sufficient to make the point that more than our school systems are at high risk, and that we are dealing with situations for which accustomed practice and organization (and their bases) are no longer adequate. Especially after World War II there were individuals (McGregor, Likert, Ruttenberg, Golden, Scanlon) who articulated criticisms of the industrial sector, predicted today's state of affairs, and recommended radical changes: in power relationships, sensitivity to personal values, incentives, and commitment. Needless to say, they were not heeded—with a few exceptions. I refer specifically to the work of Carl Frost with a number of well-known large companies. The reader who seeks more understanding of the issues together with a concrete approach to organizational change should read *The Scanlon Plan for Organizational Development: Identity, Participation, and Equity* by Frost, Wakeley, and Ruh (1974). This is not the place to review this refreshingly clear and candid work. What the reader should know is that implementation of the Scanlon Plan does not occur unless everyone in the organization has been made aware of the changes that will take place, the changes in power and responsibility that will be required, and the nature of new personal and financial incentives. Also, and crucially, the plan is not implemented unless at least 90 percent of all who are in the organization vote secretly and positively for it. It should go without saying that the organizations that have adopted the plan were hurting. They recognized that they were in trouble. Survival required that they change, and radically.[4] Unfortunately, relatively few organizational leaders have had the wisdom, courage, and vision to adopt the plan—but those who have, would now not have it any other way.

In the educational arena there is nothing comparable to the rationale, explicitness, and comprehensiveness of the Scanlon Plan. Here and there, there are schools and school systems that seek to change aspects of their organizational style and power relationships. I respect these efforts, but I have to label them as tinkering. What is becoming more frequent is the mandating by state legislatures of altered power relationships within a system and between system and community groups. That is change by fiat. I understand the frustrations and disappointments that have stimulated such mandates. If I were in the state legislature and had to vote, I would vote in favor of the mandate. But my vote would not reflect a belief that the legislation would have more than a minimal effect, if that. It would reflect my discouragement with educational administrators and policymakers who are unable or unwilling to be leaders and face up to the system's inadequacies.

I am reminded here of a public address I gave at Boston University the week after President Lyndon Johnson signed, with much fanfare, the Headstart legislation. (Initially Headstart was only a summer program.) I criticized that legislation on two grounds. First, it promised far more than it could ever achieve. Second, it was based on a theory of contagion: when underprivileged children entered school, they caught a cognitive virus that was inimical to healthy development; Headstart would inoculate them against the virus. As the years went on, it became obvious that the initial diagnosis and program were woefully inadequate. That some children would benefit by Headstart was not in question. What should have been in question was: Why should we expect that Headstart will be an adequate vaccine against the virus? What is the nature of the virus? And what does the answer to that question tell us about what changes we have to consider?

Schools, no less than private businesses, are organized human enterprises. However different their purposes seem to be, they require integration of divisions of functions. I do not take kindly to assertions that schools will improve to the extent that they adopt the presumably successful managerial style and values of the private sector. I use the word *presumably* advisedly. To imitate the private sector would be both irrelevant and another faddish disaster. That is why I have referred to the work and writings of Carl Frost, which are nothing less than an indictment of the private sector's inability to free itself from its past. But his work is valuable for two other reasons. The first is that he conceptualizes and works with the system as a whole, not this part or that part. The other is that the Scanlon Plan is essentially and explicitly an educational rationale in that it seeks to promote the personal and vocational development of everyone. I use the word *educational* because it aims to expand people's knowledge of and commitment to their individual and corporate growth. In this day and age, when we hear so much about inculcating the "right" values in our youth—well-intentioned but arid rhetoric—the Scanlon Plan gives substance to those values by making them salient to the working day, by experiencing those values in real life. John Dewey said that school is not a preparation for life, it is life. School is not a preparation for democratic living after schooling stops; it is the site for experiencing democratic living now. The Scanlon Plan is more consistent with what John Dewey said than it is with what one will observe in the modal classroom. It is no panacea. It does not rest on the assumption that the problems it addresses can be solved in the sense that four divided by two is a solution. It does not promise more than it can deliver, which is an amalgam of values, incentives, and role changes that allow problems to surface, to be discussed, and to be addressed in action in ways that are powered by commitment of all stakeholders in the enterprise. It is a clear instance of self-conscious constitution writing with its bill of rights, ultimate purposes, division of powers, checks and balances, judicial review, obligations and responsibilities, and provision for amendments. Our Federal Constitution sought to deal with an obviously inadequate Articles of Confederation, just as the Scanlon Plan is a reaction to the inadequacies of the private sector. The Founding Fathers were no tinkerers. Over a period of months in hot Philadelphia, they sought valiantly and systematically to see the whole picture—to see and limit as much as possible the unintended, adverse consequences of a myriad of proposals. They agonized. If, as they knew, they did not come up with the perfect instrument, it is because they were well aware that "solving" problems is also a process of creating problems.

I have said that any effort to reform (literally, to give new form to) our schools has to deal with the nature and allocation of power. The reader who wants a deeper understanding of what I mean should read Clinton Rossiter's fascinating *1787: The Grand Convention* (1966).

It is beyond the scope of this book to identify and discuss the different power relationships that are a feature of our school systems. There is one place in our schools where almost all of the dilemmas of power can be found. That is the classroom, which is the focus of the next chapter.

## Notes

1.  The few exceptions have gotten a good deal of play in the mass media, creating the impression that a "movement" is about. That is not the case.
2.  Timar (1989) clearly and reasonably explains why we should curb our enthusiasm about what is hoped to be gained by restructuring, the new buzzword in education. I quote the following not only to indicate briefly his conclusions based on several case studies but also because of the last three words in the quote, which refer to institutions that educational reformers seem to avoid:

> Creating a policy climate capable of fostering an integrated and organizationally coherent response to restructuring requires more than making such marginal changes as adding new programs or reshuffling organizational responsibilities. Such tinkering may actually have a negative effect on schools by embroiling them in organizational conflicts that further fragment operations and diffuse energy. An integrated response to restructuring is not likely to occur without a basic definition of the roles and responsibilities of just about every party connected with schools: teachers, administrators, professional organizations, policymakers, parents, students, and colleges and universities.

3.  The superintendent of schools in New Haven stated recently that he will present a proposal to the state legislature demanding mandatory attendance of elementary school children in return for welfare benefits to their families. (A similar proposal has already been enacted by the Wisconsin legislature.) "Right now I can guarantee a child can be

academically successful if they [sic] attended school regularly." That is quite a guarantee in light of the fact that many in the New Haven elementary schools who are from welfare families and who come regularly to school are far from academically successful. New Haven has among the highest high school dropout rates in the country, and the achievement scores of its school population are the lowest in Connecticut. This is not the place to discuss the legislation, except to say that any proposal related to schooling, especially if it has a punitive cast, that assumes that negative side effects will be minimal in frequency and consequences should be rejected. When will the reformers recognize that precisely because their recommendations are passionately held by them, their capacity seriously to consider possible harmful side effects may be impaired? When will they accompany their proposals with statements about when and how these proposals will be monitored in order to decide whether to continue or abort?

4.   In a personal communication (January 1990) Frost corrects me:

It is important to know that none of the organizations individually were hurting. It was the recognition that their industries, such as the auto-parts supply, the furniture industry, the health care industry, steel and electronics were on the threshold of domestic and global threats to their survival.

Visionary leaders seized the initiative in enabling every employee to know, to understand, and to accept the compelling realities demanding change. And once these members became literate, the leaders provided the opportunity for all the employees to become involved and responsible owners of these compelling demands for change in order to survive and to excel. This organization ownership is only realized and authenticated by the personal and professional accountability for achieving the changing competitive objectives—a fulfillment of the WE equity for common good rather than the blind-sided and selfish ME equity.

# 5

## CASE IN POINT: POWER RELATIONSHIPS IN THE CLASSROOM

POLITICAL SCIENCE CLAIMS MACHIAVELLI AS ONE OF ITS FOUN-
ders. That may come as a surprise to most people, for whom
the adjective *Machiavellian* is a pejorative signifying immorality,
deceit, and manipulativeness. The fact is that no scholar of Machiavelli regards him in such terms. What Machiavelli was concerned with was an examination of power as opportunity and
dilemma for leaders seeking the attainment of public welfare
goals. In the case of Machiavelli, that meant the unification of
Italy—that is, welding the Italian people into a sovereign nation free from domination by foreign countries who essentially
had carved up Italy into many fiefdoms. The exercise of power
for the sake of power was anathema to him. The task of an
Italian leader was to gain and use power for the Italian people,
not as a means of personal aggrandizement. It was one thing
to gain or have power—that was relatively easy, although its
costs were many; it was quite another thing to use power in
ways that would allow the people willingly to grant power. Machiavelli's advice to such a leader was based on the way things
were at that long ago time. And he pleaded with such a leader
not to confuse the way things were with what he would like

them to be. In the world of action one deals with things as they are, however seamy, complex, and problematic the context in which power has to be used. What the world could not countenance in Machiavelli was his description and analysis of the way things were and what that meant for action. Just as the world disparaged Freud because of his description of infantile sexuality—it could not believe, let alone accept, his theories—it earlier had denied validity to Machiavelli's description of the realities of power, that is, of political relationships.

If I begin this chapter with homage to Machiavelli (whom few outside of political science read), it is to make two points. The first is that the field of education has never been of much interest to political scientists, despite the fact that it is egregiously clear that schools and school systems are political organizations in which power is an organizing feature. With but a few exceptions, when political scientists have looked at schools, their descriptions and analyses have been centered on matters of policy and not on the uses and allocation of power.[1] The second point, explained in part by the first, is that the failure to examine school systems in terms of the myriad of ways in which power suffuses them has rendered efforts at reform ineffective. In no part of the school system is this failure more complete than in regard to the individual classroom.

We do not think of the classroom as a political organization. Our usual imagery of the classroom contains an adult who is "in charge" and pupils who conform to the teacher's rules, regulations, and standards. If students think and act in conformity to the teacher's wishes, they will learn what they are supposed to learn. We are not used to saying that a teacher has "power" and that students are and should be powerless. That sounds too fascistic. We are more used to saying that a teacher has authority which students should respect, precisely as those students should respect parental authority. But, as any teacher (or parent) will attest, the conventional imagery borders on fantasy. From the standpoint of the teacher, especially at the beginning of the school year and especially in the case of the beginning teacher, the name of the game is power: quickly and effectively to establish who is boss of the turf, to make it clear that the authority of the teacher is powered by the power to punish. It is no secret that the performance of the beginning teacher is viewed by his or her colleagues with bated breath. Will that teacher be able to maintain control? Will he or she be able to handle the different challenges to the teacher's authority? Will we have to come to the rescue? Is that teacher an effective disciplinarian?

Several years ago I had the opportunity to interview nine people who had begun teaching several months earlier. The focus of the interviews was on how they evaluated their training for what they experienced when they were alone in the classroom. Although the focus went far beyond matters of control or discipline, I restrict myself here only to these matters. There was unanimity on three points. First, they had been told by their mentors that establishing the authority and power of the teacher was absolutely essential. Although there was variation in what they were advised to do to achieve that goal, there was none in regard to the primacy of that goal. Second, the first few weeks of teaching were among the most stressful experiences they had ever had, far more stressful than they had expected, because they found themselves frequently on the brink of saying and doing things they knew were "psychologically wrong." Third, they feared that their inadequacies would come to the attention of the principal and other teachers—that is, those who were perceived as having power or influence to devalue them. Three of the nine teachers were still having "control problems"; the rest felt they were wrestling adequately with those problems, albeit they were omnipresent problems. All of these teachers were in New York City schools, but none of them was in what could be considered an inner-city school.

What I have related thus far is not intended to convey the impression that children are generally an unruly lot intent on making life unbearable for teachers (although some teachers might think so). Nor do I want to convey the belief that there is a way to prepare teachers for the social realities of the classroom that would prevent issues of control and power from arising. Being on one's "professional own" for the first time is inevitably stressful; in the case of teachers it is guaranteed, precisely because the establishment of their authority and power is so central to how they and others judge professional competence. The phenomenology of the beginning teacher was emphasized because it illustrates to a compelling degree what all teachers experience to a lesser degree. Power is a ubiquitous feature of classroom living. Anyone familiar with schools or the educational literature will agree that what I have described is an old story.

It is not difficult to find classrooms where issues of power and authority seem absent—that is, where the teacher and students are relaxed, the students are willingly engaged in their assigned task, and the overall ambience is friendly. If you ask these teachers to explain why this is so, they give two answers. The first is that for reasons of chance selection, no student was set to challenge the teacher's authority and power. That is to say, the students recognized and accepted the power and authority of the teacher. That power and authority were and are always silently in the picture. The second answer, usually given quickly after the first, can be put this way: "What you see now, tomorrow, this year in my classroom you may not see next year in my classroom. The students next year may be another cup of tea, a bitter brew, and I may strike you as a much less friendly, permissive, happy teacher. The dream class does not come around at all frequently. When I come to the first day of class I pray that I will not have to be a disciplinarian."

In these matters I have long felt kinship with the public school teacher. I taught at Yale for forty-four years, and within a few years after I started teaching, I came to recognize how remarkably different successive cohorts of first-year graduate students could be in terms of motivation, intellectual curiosity and, yes, challenges (hostile or otherwise) to my authority. There were years when in class I could sit back after some opening remarks and act as moderator of heated discussions. There were years when getting a discussion going was almost impossible. There were years when a student or two made it clear, by oral or body language, that they did not highly regard the substance and style of my teaching. One thing that was always in the picture for both the students and me was that I had to grade them, and the grade I gave them could be fateful for their professional futures as well as their status in the department. I had power and I and they knew it; that brute fact governed both of us. It was no less a problem for me than it was for them, although it is safe to assume that they did not see this as a problem for me. If we are not accustomed to think of the public school classroom in political terms—in terms of the nature and consequences of power where power is asymmetrically allocated—we are similarly unaccustomed to think of the university classroom in those terms. Unaccustomed, that is, until the dynamics of that power explode into full view, as happened in the sizzling sixties in the university, secondary schools, and every other major societal institution. If educators in our schools and universities were taken by surprise at this challenge to their authority and power, it was because they had never had reason to view or question how institutions in which they were embedded—in and to which they had been socialized—were implicitly and silently based on power and relationships waiting to surface.

Just as teachers are extraordinarily alert to issues of power—sensitive to behavior that may or will require exercise of power, as well as to individual differences among students—so are the students. If substitute teachers have control problems, it says as much about the knowledgeability of students about power as it does about the substitutes' unfamiliarity with the traditions of their classrooms and the casts of characters. Issues of power are always a function of the perceptions and actions of student *and* teacher. Here is an extreme example. In the course of working in classrooms in an inner-city school, I saw a nine-year-old boy literally climb the wall. The school was almost a hundred years old and the steam pipes were exposed, enabling the youngster to climb to the ceiling. His teacher was utterly inadequate to handle him and others in that classroom. I said to the boy: "Next year you will be in Mrs. Esposito's classroom. Is that the way you will act there?" With practically no reaction time, he replied: "I would never do it in *her* classroom. She would kick the shit out of me."

How does power get defined in the classroom? What understanding of power do we want children to obtain? Should students have some kind of role in defining power, thus giving them some sense of ownership not only in regard to definition but also to implementation? Is the unilateral definition and exercise of power desirable for the development of children? Does it tend to breed the opposite of what it intends to achieve?

It was these kinds of questions that stimulated me to do the following. In several elementary school classrooms I arranged for observers to be there from the first day of school to the end of the month. I was after what I described as the forging of the classroom's "constitution." What were the rules and regulations that governed the classroom and how were they arrived at? The task of the observers was to record and describe any instance relevant to the articulation of rules and regulations: when and how these instances arose and who was involved. Who wrote the constitution of the classroom? The answer—to which there was no exception—was that the teachers wrote the constitution. They articulated the rules and regulations (frequently post hoc) but provided no rationale. There was absolutely no discussion about the rationale. It was as if the teachers, Moses-like, came down from Mt. Sinai with the constitution. (The response of the Israelites, remember, was far from warm.) It never occurred to these teachers, who by conventional standards were very good, that students should be provided with a rationale, which deserved extended discussion, and that students should have the opportunity to voice their opinions. How should we live together and why? These were suburban classrooms to which almost all students came with respect for teachers—that is, they knew that they were expected to conform to the teacher's rules and regulations, or else. In these matters it was as if teachers had no respect for the needs and opinions of students. Students were and should be powerless in these matters. Their time would come when they "grew up." In all but one or two of these classrooms, there were clear examples of rule formulation or rule implementation to which some of the students did not take kindly. They never received clarifying discussion.

It is ironic that today we hear much about how unfair it is

that teachers are powerless to influence policies (read: constitution) that mightily affect them. As I write these words, the metropolitan mass media are giving a lot of play to the new chancellor-designate of the New York City school system who, as head of the Dade County school system in Florida, has empowered teachers (and others) in formulating policies for their schools. In a television interview, Dr. Fernandez stated that "the evidence is not yet in" about whether what he has done in Dade County will have the intended desirable consequences. He was unambiguous, however, in stating that for teachers to be held accountable for educational outcomes required that they have more power than tradition has accorded them. To state it oxymoronically, Fernandez is a skeptical utopian. The media are giving a good deal of play to the criticism directed to Fernandez by the head of the administrator's union, who regard teachers the way teachers regard students. And therein is the irony: teachers regard students the way their superiors regard them—that is, as incapable of dealing responsibly with issues of power, even on the level of discussion. The head of the administrator's union does not say that teachers have to grow up to handle power because if he did, he would have to face the question: how do you grow up in or to a role in which you are denied experience or access? When do you start? It is no different in the case of the student in the classroom. When should students begin to experience the nature and dilemmas of power in group living?

I have focused on the classroom not to make the obvious point that power is one of its distinctive features but to suggest that the sense of powerlessness frequently breeds reduced interest and motivation, at best a kind of passionless conformity and at worst a rejection of learning. When one has no stake in the way things are, when one's needs or opinions are provided no forum, when one sees oneself as the object of unilateral actions, it takes no particular wisdom to suggest that one would rather be elsewhere. We are used to hearing today that too many students lack interest, motivation, and intellectual curiosity. An explanation is by no means simple, but surely one of its ingredients is the fact that schools are uninteresting places for many students (and teachers). I discussed this at some length in my book *Schooling in America: Scapegoat and Salvation* (1983). Here I wish only to emphasize that if classrooms are uninteresting places, it is in part (and only in part) because students feel, and are made to feel, powerless to influence the traditional regularities of the classroom. One of the regularities is that determining what is right and wrong, just and fair, is solely in the province of the teacher and completely off limits to students. Teachers are legislators, executives, and judiciary. Underlying this behavioral regularity is the assumption that students are incapable of exercising power responsibly in any way or on any level. Furthermore, it is dangerous to accord them power.

Here is an example. I was sitting in a first-grade classroom in an elementary school. The new school year had begun a week earlier. One child was sitting in her seat, head down, crying silently. Occasionally, the child would slowly approach the teacher and nestle against her. The teacher would then take the child back to her seat, saying sympathetically: "When school is over, your mother will come for you. Stay in your seat and try to do what the other students are doing." Later the teacher told me that each day the child cried when the mother brought her to school. What the child wanted, the teacher said, was to be held, cuddled, and soothed. My conversation with the teacher went something like this:

*SBS:*   The girl asked to be held?

*T:*   Yes. She would raise her hands for me to pick her up.

*SBS:*   Did you?

*T:*   No.

*SBS:*   Why not?

*T:*   (with a surprised look) If I picked her up and cuddled her, then that is what other children would want me to do for them.

*SBS:*  In other words, the other children would want to get in on the act?

*T:*  You are so right!

*SBS:*  (after a long pause) What if you were to discuss this with your class? What if you were to explain to them that Gail misses her mother terribly and that is why she is so unhappy and wants to be picked up and held by you. What should a teacher do in such a case? Should she accede to the child's needs and wishes? I am willing to bet that their answer would be a definite yes. And what if you were to say that what you would do for Gail you are prepared to do for others who would feel about leaving their mothers as Gail does?

The anecdote illustrates two related points. The first is that discussing the dilemma with the class was foreign to this teacher's conception of her role, which is that she does not take up such issues with students, and that she alone decides what is the right course of action. Second, she feels that these young children are incapable of understanding, let alone articulating, the issues involved. Indeed, it would be dangerous to discuss the matter because what they might say is unpredictable. Leave well enough alone.

It would be a gross misunderstanding of what I am suggesting if it conjured up imagery of a classroom in which the teacher is a market researcher seeking to determine what children want her or him to do. It would be no less wrong if the reader concluded that I am suggesting that teachers give up the power to make final decisions. What I am advocating is that the teacher should accord students the right *and* responsibility to participate in forums where the constitution of the classroom is forged. The classroom should be a place where those in it come to feel that they will be governed by rules and values they have had an opportunity to discuss. The overarching goal is not to come up with rules but to begin to comprehend the complexities of power in a complicated group setting. Put another way, the goal is to instill in students an understanding of a commitment to the classroom constitution, a sense of ownership, and an awareness that their opinions will be respected, even when not accepted.

For purposes of this discussion, I divide the world of parents into two groups, one far smaller than the other. The small group comprises those parents set to be sensitive to and respectful of the opinions of their children, not in order to go along with them but rather to determine with what they are dealing. These are parents who seek to avoid adversarialism and the need to exercise naked power. They are prepared to compromise but not to surrender. They know when and how to "flex," to take risks, and also to put their foot down. Inside this cake of virtue are, among other things, anxiety, puzzlement, indecision, and ambivalence. What appears on the surface is one thing; what goes on inside is far more volatile and even confused. But whatever goes on inside does not prevent these parents from listening to, respecting, and mulling over what their children are saying and requesting, or demanding. Just as the children know that their parents have power—of this the children have no doubt—the parents have no doubt that their children have power to affect them. What the parents seek is a modus vivendi with which both "great powers" can live.

The much larger group consists of parents who are, if not polar opposites, on different points of the continuum. The polar opposites are those parents for whom unilaterally exercised power creates what one part of them seeks to avoid. The great powers are in struggle.

Teachers are kin to parents, which is why so many of them experience their students in terms of a power struggle. In recent years the term *parenting* has gained a good deal of currency. Courses in parenting are becoming part of the secondary school and college curriculum. And, especially since World War II, the number of books published on parenting seems to be increasing exponentially; at some future date there may be more such books than there are parents. This social phenomenon says a good deal about how problematic parenting has become. It is astonishing, however, that parenting in the classroom—not as a technical but as a fundamental set of issues fateful for learning and growth—has received virtually no recognition or discussion in any of the many commission reports on educational reform. When these reports say anything, it is to affirm "law and order" in the classroom, an affirmation of the traditional view that the power to govern resides solely in the teacher. As I said to a commission member: "No one is opposed to law and order. What should be at issue is how laws arise and how order is experienced and, fatefully, how those processes contribute to productive learning and desirable social living. None of your recommendations speaks to that issue, as if the basis for life in the classroom is in no way an object of scrutiny and reform." He looked at me as if I were one of those bleeding-heart sentimentalists whose misguided ideas deserve no response. I later learned that he described me as being in the John Dewey tradition. He was, of course, absolutely correct. I would bet, and give very attractive odds, that he never read anything by John Dewey. Sloganeering as a defense against the acquisition of knowledge is all too frequent.[2]

There is another reason I have focused on the classroom in this chapter. After reading the reports on educational reform, I had to conclude that they were written by people who either had only the foggiest notion of what goes on in classrooms or who had once been or taught in the classroom but had amnesia for what they had experienced. For example, in no report— and it is no less true in the general education literature—is anything said about question-asking behavior in the classroom. Why question-asking behavior? The answer in brief is that humans are very distinctive question-asking organisms, and question asking is not only a reflection of curiosity but also one of the royal roads to productive knowledge and action. It is surprising how little attention has been given to this characteristic in educational research and the preparation of educational personnel. If the research is scanty, it is extraordinarily compelling and unanimous in findings. In the modal classroom (for example, a social studies period of forty minutes) the average number of questions asked by students is two, and those two questions could have been asked by one student. Teachers' rate of question asking varies from about 40 to 150. No one, including developmentalists and teachers, to whom the findings of this research have been presented has ever said that these are desirable results. It is beyond my purposes to explain this regularity in any detail. But it does suggest, central to my present purposes, that students do not feel secure in exercising the right or power to ask questions. Indeed, too frequently, students fear asking questions—testimony again to the role of power in classroom living. And when fear is not a factor—and I do not want to overplay its frequency—it is because students accept or conform to their perception of the rules of the game implicitly or explicitly set by the teacher. And yet, in the scores of recommendations for educational reform, no question is ever raised about question asking. The explicit ultimate goal of all of these recommendations is to improve educational outcomes. The assumption undergirding these recommendations seems to be that those outcomes can be achieved without any significant alteration in the behavioral-constitutional-social regularities of the modal classroom. It is an assumption as obfuscating as it is invalid. One can change curricula, standards, and a lot of other things by legislation or fiat, but if the regularities of the classroom remain unexamined and unchanged, the failure of the reforms is guaranteed.

What responsibility in the classroom are students given for their learning? As I have indicated, the student's responsibility is an individual one: to do, by himself or herself, the tasks assigned by the teacher. Indeed, it is implicit, and frequently explicit, that students work by themselves. What assumptions undergird this regularity? One assumption is that students are generally incapable of working in a cooperative, productive way with other students. A second assumption is that even if that incapability is unjustified, the products that emerge from small-group activity do not permit evaluation of individual contributions—that is, individual contributions are "ungradable." A third assumption is that the dynamics of power in such groups can be anti-educational for many students. The exercise of power in the classroom is a feature not only of teacher-student relationships; it is no less a feature of student-student relationships, which, it is assumed, can get out of hand in small task-oriented groups. These assumptions, singly or in combination, justify the present regularity, which seems so right, natural, and proper. How classroom learning is structured is a derivative of the power of the teacher. That means that the teacher has the power to alter, even radically, how learning is structured. He or she can decide, in regard to any subject matter or task, to structure things differently—for example, to form small groups each of which is given responsibility to do the task as it sees fit. The nature of the task is clear; how the small group meets the task is its responsibility. The members of the groups are given the power to organize themselves as they see fit. They are given a degree of power, of control. That does not mean that the teacher sits by passively unavailable for help and advice, but that each small group has been given responsibility for and control over its outcomes.

I do not bring up these considerations only to emphasize again the sources and exercise of power in the classroom. Another reason is to note that in recent decades there has been a growing research literature comparing two kinds of classrooms: those in which the teacher conventionally teaches the whole class, and those in which teachers have been trained in the organization and supervision of classrooms where students have been organized into small groups (cooperative learning). One major conclusion that can be drawn from this research literature is that where cooperative learning is implemented, classrooms do not become disorganized, disorganizing, and chaotic places. Law and order are not replaced by anarchy or mob behavior. This is not to say that peace and quiet reign supreme, but the expectation that students will mischievously misuse and subvert their groups is not realized. A second conclusion is that the level of student interest and motivation is far higher than in the usual "whole class" method of teaching. A third conclusion is that using the criterion of academic achievement, the cooperative, small-group approach is as effective as the conventional one and, more often than not, is superior. A final conclusion is that, depending on the particular focus of the research study and the outcome measures used, the small-group method changes racial and ethnic attitude in a desirable direction. Despite these findings, there is no evidence that they are influencing either the preparation of teachers or classroom practice.[3]

The small-group method is no panacea. We do not, at this time, know its limitations. It is not being paraded, nor should it be, as the answer to the improvement of educational outcomes. But in two crucial respects this literature is refreshing indeed. I refer, first, to its focus on life in the classroom, the place where all of the intended goals of educational reform are to be influential. And it is a literature that explicitly holds that how life and learning in the classroom is structured makes a difference, and that the existing structure is ineffective—more accurately, it is part of the problem and not the solution. Secondly, the proponents of the small-group method leave no doubt that implementing the method requires the unlearning of conventional attitudes, practices, and assumptions and the learning of new ones, a difficult task for anyone. It cannot be achieved by fiat or simply high motivation. It requires literally a re-education, which these researchers do not gloss over. In several studies the efforts of the researchers just to prepare teachers for implementation approached the heroic. In fact, in reading this literature one has to keep in mind that participating teachers were almost always volunteers. Even so, life was not easy for them. Changing the regularities in the classroom is a very complex, demanding, and personally upsetting affair even when motivation is high.[4] (People who willingly enter psychotherapy to change regularities in their thinking and actions know what I mean. If love is not enough, neither is motivation.) When I read this literature, which inevitably varies in quality, I am always reminded of what happened in the sixties and seventies when educational policymakers legislated the wholesale introduction of the new math, the new biology, the new physics, the new social studies, and a lot of other new things. They were scandalously insensitive to what was involved in changing classroom regularities. Teachers had to teach a new curricula, usually after a workshop of several days, as unrealistic a time perspective as has ever been employed. It was as if teaching the new curricula was a technical or engineering task that could be learned in short order by any biologically intact teacher. Like today's educational reformers, their grasp of life in the classroom was, to put it charitably, unknowledgeable.

Let us return for a moment to children's question asking: When do you not answer a child's question but rather help the child use his or her resources to get an answer? Obviously, if you think the child is capable of finding an answer, you should encourage him or her to do so. Because a child asks a question is no reason automatically to provide an answer. How you respond should depend in part on your assessment of how much responsibility a child can assume for pursuing an answer. Generally speaking, in and out of the classroom, we underestimate the capability of children to pursue answers on their own. We respond as if they are irresponsible in this regard, and we usually end up proving the self-fulfilling prophecy. One of the major sources of resistance to the use of cooperative learning is the assumption that students are incapable of taking some responsibility for their learning.

If in this chapter I have focused on certain aspects of power relationships in the classroom, it is because these aspects say a great deal about conceptions of the responsibility that students can or should assume for learning. In the modal classroom the degree of responsibility given to students is minimal. They are responsible only in the sense that they are expected to complete tasks assigned by teachers and in ways the teachers have indicated. They are not responsible to other students. They are solo learners and performers responsible to one adult. They are expected to be rugged individualists. Implicitly and explicitly, the task of the teacher is to foster that individualism. When we are told that the overarching aim of schooling is to help each child realize his or her full potential, it engenders the imagery of *a* child and *a* teacher, the latter zealously concentrating on the former. The responsibility of the teacher, a derivative of his or her power, is awesome. It is also unrealistic and unjustified. Unrealistic because it is impossible, as any teacher will attest, to do justice to the needs and talents of each child in the classroom, a source of guilt in many teachers. It is unjustified because it rests on the unexamined and invalid assumption that there are not alternative and productive ways of structuring the social context in which learning can occur, ways that give more responsibility to students. For example, consider a recent modest but seminal study by Mehan (1989). Microcomputers were given to four elementary school teachers, and changes in classroom organization, teacher-student relations, and curriculum were observed over a period of a year. Overall, Mehan found that the teachers fitted "their new microcomputers into previously established classroom organizational practices; they seldom modified spatial and temporal arrangements." Two of the teachers taught by the "whole class" method; two employed a method that could be subsumed under "cooperative learning." Although each teacher adapted the microcomputer into his or her customary style of organizing the classroom, all of them placed two students together at the computer. What is noteworthy is that these computers were tied in with a student newswire service known as the "Computer Chronicles."

> The Computer Chronicles Newswire is an electronic network that connects students from Alaska, California, Hawaii, Israel, and Mexico. Students from each of these locations write and edit articles stored on floppy disks. Information on the disks is sent to all sites participating in the network. Students at each site use the articles they have written as well as ones written by students elsewhere in the network to produce their local editions of the "Computer Chronicles Newspaper." The network is explicitly modeled on the international news wire services. Whenever possible, students' attention is focused on the parallels between their work and the work of newspaper editors and reporters.
>
> The Computer Chronicles helped the teachers establish learning environments that were functional, that is, reading and writing were organized for communicative purposes and not just as an exercise for teachers to evaluate. The presence of an audience for writing, in the form of classmates, parents, and peers in distant places, was a cru-

cial ingredient in making the Computer Chronicles a functional system for reading and writing. Having an audience with which students were unable to communicate verbally, but with which they wanted to share ideas, gave students a purpose for writing. This writing for a purpose and not writing for teacher evaluation or even to work on the computer, subordinated students' concern for the mechanics of writing to the goal of communicating clearly.

When the students realized that other people would read their work for the information they provided and not just to evaluate its form, they took more control of their writing. They engaged actively in revising and editing their own writing and the texts of their peers. After students wrote and edited their articles for the newswire, the articles were submitted to a local editorial board for consideration. If the local editorial board, composed of five to eight students, accepted an article, then it appeared in the classroom newspaper and was read by the author's family and friends.

Articles were also sent over the newswire to other schools, where other students reviewed their work and decided whether to include it in their local newspapers. If accepted in these remote locations, then not only local peers, but people in Alaska, Hawaii, and Mexico read their work. This goal of writing for an audience was extremely effective in motivating both reading and writing [Mehan, 1989].

Mehan concludes:

When the introduction of microcomputers did not modify existing spatial and temporal arrangements, their availability co-occurred with a new participation structure in the classroom. Teachers placed two students together at the computer. Peer interaction emerged from this arrangement. Students worked together at computers without direct adult supervision. They were left to their own devices to sort out the manner in which tasks would be completed. While students were responsible for completing their assigned work at computers, the students worked out the details of task completion themselves, resulting in voluntary instead of compulsory forms of instruction activity. Since the teachers did not monitor the students' work at the computer directly, their work was evaluated privately instead of publicly. As a consequence of this change in participation structures, students developed a different sense of social relations. They assisted each other at the computer and cooperated to complete assigned tasks.

On a nationally normed language arts test, all classes showed gains, but those gains were most pronounced in the classrooms of the two teachers who had organized students in a cooperative learning mode. Mehan makes clear that he does not claim that the word processors are responsible for improved writing: "The computer by itself is not an agent of change. In and of themselves, word processing systems cannot teach children to read and write. While we have found that word processing systems cannot transform unskilled writers into skilled ones, they do have properties that enable teachers to make a new social organization for reading and writing possible. It is this social organization and not the microcomputer that changed both what was taught and the way in which it was taught in the project classrooms." In Mehan's study it was a social organization that gave students more control over what and how they learned. Unfortunately, the myriad of proposals for educational reform are thunderingly silent on issues of social organization in the classroom.

In the previous chapter I briefly described the work of Carl Frost in applying the Scanlon Plan in small and large business organizations (including health care ones). I mention it again here in order to emphasize one of its central features: the formation of small groups given responsibility for formulating plans, advice, and goals, a degree of responsibility and power they never were accorded before. If you think the employee is incapable of being more responsible in regard to the goals of an organization, it is likely that you will use daily experience as proof of these expectations. It is no different in the case of teachers in a school who are customarily viewed precisely the way the teachers view children. And it is no different in the case of most middle-management school administrators who are accorded authority with little or no real responsibility. The social organization of the modal classroom is quite representative of the social organization of the school and the school system. Given the underlying assumptions, it cannot be otherwise.

Nothing in what I have said should be interpreted as suggesting that any alternative conception of social organization is a "solution": state its rationale clearly, write up a detailed training manual, and an unsatisfactory state of affairs will be remedied. If I intended to convey anything, it is that the traditional mode of classroom organization, as well as that of the school and school system, creates rather than dilutes problems that adversely affect or greatly constrict the productivity of all participants in the educational arena. What we have now is not working to anyone's satisfaction. All efforts over the past several decades to improve the situation have failed, and, I have to predict, efforts to implement current reforms will end in failure as well. If there is a single message I have tried to convey, it is that alternatives to present practice have to be tried, and by practice I mean not only what observation allows us to see and describe but also the baggage of implicit assumptions underlying practice. We have had a surfeit of band-aid reforms. Band-aids are functional when the biological health of an organism is not a problem, but when that organism is systemically unsound and you apply the band-aid to a manifestation of that unsoundness, your intentions may be praiseworthy (and you deserve an A) but your understanding of what you are confronting deserves no praise (and you should get an F). In regard to our schools, there is too much at stake to refrain from passing judgment.

### Notes

1. One of the exceptions is Willis Hawley. His article on the commentary page of *Education Week* for November 1,

1989—in the form of an imaginary conversation with the president of the country taking office in 1993—is a concise summary of many thoughts discussed in this book. I knew Hawley a couple of decades ago when he was immersed in the development and study of an alternative public school in New Haven. He learned the game and he knows the score. I also recommend an earlier article by Hawley (1988).

2.  It is appropriate here to say that many of the issues I discuss in this book are explicitly or implicitly contained in John Dewey's writings on education. Also, anyone who reads Alfred North Whitehead's *The Aims of Education,* a collection of essays published in 1929, will quickly see why he was so influential in my thinking. That will become more apparent when, at the end of this book, I present what I call the overarching education we should have for students. One of my favorite sentences in Whitehead is: "In training a child to activity of thought, above all things we must beware of what I call 'inert ideas'—that is to say, ideas that are merely received into the mind without being utilized, or tested, or thrown into fresh combinations." Also: "Except at rare intervals of intellectual ferment, education in the past has been radically infested with inert ideas. That is the reason uneducated, clever women, who have seen much of the world, are in middle life so much the most cultured part of the community. They have been saved from this horrible burden of inert ideas." That, of course, was said long before the women's liberation movement really gained momentum, and one has to ask whether today women have the same burden of inert ideas as men!

3.  The reader who wishes to become familiar with this research literature should read the following, each of which contains a more extensive reading list: Johnson and Johnson (1987); Johnson, Johnson, and Maruyama (1983); Sharan (1980); Sharan and others (1984); Slavin, 1983.

4.  To introduce teachers *and* a school to cooperative learning is no easy task. Introduction is easy but implementation is not, because it encounters a host of predictable problems deriving from the nature of the school culture. The most

succinct and sophisticated account I have read of the process is a chapter by Sharan and Sharan in a forthcoming book, *Current Perspectives on School Culture,* edited by Nancy Wyner.

# 6

## OBSTACLES TO CHANGE

HOW, WHEN, AND WHY NEW IDEAS GAIN CURRENCY, GET AC-
cepted and institutionally implemented, are questions far beyond the purposes of this book. A modest-sized library could
be easily filled with the books written on the subject. A fair
proportion of these books would be disheartening to read because they chronicle new ideas that have all of the transitory
and superficial features of fads and fashions. That is clearly
the case in the educational arena, where new ideas have not
been in short supply among those within and without the educational establishment. And, in too many cases, where the new
ideas deserved consideration, the processes through which they
were implemented were self-defeating. Ideas whose time has
come are no guarantee that we know how to capitalize on the
opportunities, because the process of implementation requires
an understanding of the settings in which these ideas have to
take root. That understanding is frequently faulty and incomplete. Good intentions married to good ideas are necessary but
not sufficient for action consistent with them. In accordance
with Murphy's Law, if anything can go wrong it will. The world
is not organized in ways that permit it passively to conform to

our needs or good ideas, and when that fact interacts with our capacity to oversimplify, and even to delude ourselves, disappointment is not far down the road. That explains Sullivan's Law: Murphy's Law is a gross underestimation.

These musings are prologue to a brief recounting of some experiences I have had which may help the reader understand a few of the factors that either facilitate or obstruct efforts at reform—in other words, why some ideas never get a hearing and others do. The first three examples do not involve schools; the last two do. At the very least, these examples should disabuse the reader of the belief that obstacles to change are more frequent and serious in educational institutions than in other types of settings.

The first example does not stem from personal experience. It is about a dramatic change that took place two or three decades ago in the treatment of heart attacks. Heretofore, a person who suffered a heart attack was kept on bed rest in the hospital for several weeks. Patients were led to believe that any physical exertion off the bed might bring on another heart attack. Bed rest meant just that: stay in bed until there was evidence that the process of repair was well along. It is quite a different story today, where the patient may be gotten up and about just days after entering the hospital. Now, this dramatic change in practice did not come about overnight because someone wrote a paper pointing out that prolonged bed rest could be inimical to recovery, indeed could produce lethal side effects. As one would expect, physicians, who had been taught about the necessity of prolonged bed rest, were not about to do a flip-flop. No less than their patients, physicians feared changing their practices. And, of course, there were those who ignored the new practice as medical nonsense and irresponsibility. The point is that what today we regard as factual was factual then but not regarded as such.

Acceptance and change did not come about merely by the passage of time or simply by the impact of published studies. The growing body of evidence was clearly a factor, but so was the prestige of the medical centers that had changed and evaluated the new practice. Even so, in thousands of hospitals it took leadership and persuasion, and possibly at times coercion, to get physicians to change their methods. If tomorrow morning a prestigious medical journal were to publish an article demonstrating that a particular form of cancer had been arrested or cured by a new drug, it is safe to assume that physicians would clamor to get and use the drug, and patients would be beating at their doors. Such a drug fits in with the belief system and practices of physicians, just as it fits in with the hopes of patients. That was not the case with heart attacks; physicians and patients were fearful of this change because it contradicted their belief systems and customary practice. Physicians did not change quickly, and being required to get off the bed after several days is still experienced by patients as intuitively dangerous.

The passage of time and the dissemination of findings are insufficient as explanations of a change in practice, either its acceptance or pace. No less important are the nature and strength of belief systems of people embedded in organizations whose culture structure and traditions vary considerably in regard to change. And it makes a difference if the change in institutional practice has a voluntary feature, even though that feature may not be free of reluctance or the anxiety engendered by risk taking or the perception that one has to roll with the punches. Educational reformers have trouble understanding that change by legislative fiat or policy pronouncements from on high is only the first and the easiest step in the change process, a step that sets in motion the dynamic of problem creation through problem solution. Content to remain on that first step, assuming as they do that the goals of change can be achieved by a process that could be called human mechanical engineering, insensitive as they are to what the change will activate in the phenomenology of individuals and their institutional relationships, they confuse a change in policy with a change in practice. And they also assume that change is achieved through learning and applying new or good ideas. They seem unable to understand what is involved in unlearning what custom, tradition, and even research have told educational personnel is right, natural, and proper. So, if physicians did not one day as a group willingly give up complete bed rest as treatment for a heart attack, it should occasion no surprise.

The second example stems from personal experience in connection with the creation of the first rooming-in unit in an American hospital. This took place during World War II and the effort was spearheaded by Edith Jackson, a child psychoanalyst, and Grover Powers, head of Yale's Department of Pediatrics and a world-renowned figure. (He trained more heads of pediatric departments than anyone before or since.) It was conventional practice that after delivery the mother was taken to her room and the infant was put in the nursery. The infant was brought to the mother's room for feeding and then returned to the nursery. The rationale, in brief, for this practice was: the mother was too exhausted from pregnancy and delivery to care personally for the infant; the mother did not want to deal with the needs and problems of the newborn; the practice was efficient in terms of the time demands on nurses and physicians; and, of course, the practice protected the infant against external bacteria and viruses. (Today it is not unusual for mother and child to leave the hospital after two or three days. In those days, staying in the hospital a week to ten days was not unusual; it was thought that the mother needed that time to recover her strength.)

The rationale for rooming-in was: for many mothers separation from their newborn engendered all kinds of anxiety and fantasies about how the child was being treated (not responding to its crying, no fondling, failure to recognize a problem, unwitting switching of name tags); the separation delayed or interfered with a crucial "bonding" process between mother and infant; some mothers resented having to conform to a feeding schedule and wished to breast-feed the infant on demand, that is, when she felt feeding was necessary; having the child in the same room with the mother could be an educational experience in infant care, especially if this was the mother's first child; nursing and medical personnel could have a salutary and anxiety-reducing educational role; rooming-in should be available to those mothers who wanted it; rooming-in would also facilitate a more active, hands-on role for the father; rooming-in would reduce the frequency of untoward psychological stress associated with the discontinuity between the hospital experience and being at home.

It is obvious, I trust, that what Jackson and Powers wanted to create was an alternative to institutional custom and practice. It was not only an alternative but it was also an implicit criticism of existing practice. I say implicit because Jackson and Powers sedulously tried to keep it so. This they did by emphasizing that they wished to study and evaluate rooming-in—that is, as a research project. Were not the Yale Medical School and associated hospital in the business of contributing to knowledge? Did not such a research effort fit in with their mission? Other than by challenging existing practice and trying out and studying promising alternatives (rooming-in had been created and studied by Grantly Dick Read in England), how could existing practice get changed? Finally, Grover Powers was no Johnny-come-lately to medical research and proactive health care. His credentials were impeccable, and he was a powerful person in the Yale Medical School.

The fact was that rooming-in and customary practice rested on dramatically different conceptions of mothers, fathers, infants, and families. The proponents for rooming-in lived in a very different psychological world than those wedded to existing practice. Jackson and Powers knew that, and they anticipated problems of acceptance in both principle and implementation. Perhaps because both of them were excruciatingly interpersonally sensitive, gracious people, both on the surface meek and quiet individuals, both utterly incapable of the hard sell, they underestimated what they would be up against. (As it turned out, the cast of characters in this drama vastly underestimated the strength of Powers and Jackson's resolve, personal strength, persistence, and patience.)

It would be an exaggeration to say that I observed internecine struggle, but not much of an exaggeration. Civility was not breached. If it was not sweetness and light, neither was it open warfare. It is said that war is a continuation of politics by other means. In this case politics, a word I do not use pejoratively, was a means to prevent war.

Why the strife? Consider three facts. First, the project required commitments from the Department of Obstetrics and Gynecology, hospital nurses, the School of Nursing, and hospital administrators. It also required new space (and, as usual, space was at a premium). Second, it required the cooperation of community obstetricians and pediatricians, whose patients would request rooming-in. And third, it required more than the cooperation of all of these individuals and units; it required them to change their thinking and practice—that is, to unlearn the old and to struggle to adapt appropriately to the new. In brief, Jackson and Powers were spearheading an institutional change, a change in the allocation of power and responsibility, in no way different from implementing a major change in a school or school system. Programmatic and behavioral regularities would have to change if goals were to be achieved.

What were the factors that contributed to the creation of the rooming-in unit? And what do they suggest about why almost all efforts of change in a school system fail? The first factor was the time perspective of Jackson and Powers. However much they desired to set an opening date, they knew that goal to be unrealistic because of the discussions, negotiations, and problems the project brought to the fore. The rooming-in unit could not be created by fiat. If in principle it could have been so created, the result would have been an institutional and personal disaster. The needs, attitudes, self-interests, and idiosyncrasies of the relevant individuals and departments had to be respected and dealt with, not ignored, decided, or cavalierly dismissed. The goal was not token cooperation but personal commitment, and that would take time and patience. That Jackson and Powers wished it otherwise, that there were times they wanted to throw in the towel goes without saying. Their time perspective was governed by social and institutional realities; it was not predetermined. This is in marked contrast to efforts at educational change that plan and implement change by the calendar and frequently by fiat. There shall be changes in September when school begins! That is like the teacher who says that by October 15 we *will* be on page 22. You can begin change on September 15 and you can be on page 22 on October 15. But at what cost for whom at what price? There have been too many educational reformers who know the cost of everything and the value of nothing.

This is not the place to go into all of the factors that made for the creation and implementation of the rooming-in unit, which by research findings was successful (albeit not wholly) and stimulated the creation of such units around the country. There are two related factors that must be mentioned, however, and they concern leadership. The first, and the more obvious of the two, was that Jackson and Powers had courage, an unstudied concept in psychology, to take on a soul-searching and soul-trying project because they believed that it was in the best interests of infants and parents. Believing as they did, they could not walk away from intervening and experimenting. If existing practice had its defects, they were duty bound to do something about it. The second factor largely concerns Powers. Although a rooming-in unit was initially Jackson's idea, Powers not only bought the idea but committed himself to it wholeheartedly. As I have said, no one at the Yale Medical School was held in higher respect than he was. (The truth is that Jackson was not held in high regard because she was both a psychiatrist and a psychoanalyst, and neither in those days was held in esteem, especially in medical schools. Besides, Jackson was far from an articulate individual.) The point is that Powers did not stop at giving his blessings to the project. As someone near or at the top of the administrative pyramid, he did not say: "It's a good idea. I'll let everybody know about my support, so go ahead and get started." I have seen scores of educational policymakers who had what they thought was a good idea, or said they would support someone who did, who left it to less powerful or less knowledgeable or less committed people to initiate and sustain the implementation process. This style of leadership, especially in regard to a major change, almost always (in my experience) produces two effects: implementation subverts original intent, and those on the firing line, the teachers, end up saying: "He (or she) was ignorant of what was involved, what really happened, and why nothing really has changed." Powers not only carried the ball but he was also his own interference. He accepted responsibility and that meant that he was, had to be, an active participant: explaining, arguing, cajoling, persisting, persuading, and making it clear how much the project meant to him. Undoubtedly, he offered carrots but it is also the case that others knew that he would not use his stick. Using the stick was inconsistent with his personal style and bedrock values.

I do not expect leaders of complex organizations, of which a school system is but one example, to get very involved in every effort at change. But when the change is obviously major, a challenging alternative to the status quo, one that asks of people that they change their thinking and practice, that change requires the leader to go beyond pronouncement and blessings. Unless, as is too frequently the case, the leader is truly ignorant of what the proposed change requires. And unless the leader confuses power with influence. Powers understood the difference. To expect people to accept an alternative way of thinking and practicing rests on a psychology guaranteed to maximize failure. It is a very common psychology that has only one virtue for this type of leader: it makes it easy to assign blame for failure to others.

The third example of the difficulty in entertaining, let alone accepting, alternative ways of thinking and practicing is not an institutional one in the narrow sense. From one standpoint, this example could be described as an instance of the disregard of available evidence. From another standpoint, it could be described as an extreme form of professional parochialism, involving as it does in this instance an entire medical specialty: its practitioners and their professional-educational preparation. One might say that it is an example of how an educational system in this country prevented its students from acquiring knowledge of what was going on in their specialty in another country.

It was during the mid-life of the Yale Psycho-Educational Clinic in the sixties. At one of our weekly meetings we tried to bring in nonpsychologists who had an interest in, or in their fields took part in, the change process. To one of these meet-

ings I invited Edward Cohart, an internationally respected
physician and epidemiologist in Yale's Department of Public
Health in the medical school. He was a friend whom I respected for many reasons, not least of which was an unexcelled
ability to come up with alternative explanations of research
findings as well as alternative suggestions to customary practice. He presented two sets of findings. The first was the customary surgical treatment of breast cancer in the United States:
its rationale, methods, and outcomes as they had been re-
ported in the research literature. The second was the same information for England. In the United States at that time the
procedure employed most was radical mastectomy. In England
radical mastectomy was by no means common; lumpectomy or
similarly less invasive surgery was much preferred. In terms of
outcomes, however, there was no difference between the two
approaches. Indeed, the evidence suggested that the less invasive procedures may have had better outcomes.

Today in the United States radical mastectomy is much less
frequent than heretofore. This change did not come about
without opposition or controversy. Indeed, the controversy
continues today. I am not competent to judge the complexities
of the issues, but as a surgical friend said to me: "Complexities
aside, no one in this country now denies that what was established treatment should not have been so established. Surgeons
and oncologists were not ignorant of British practice and findings. But they were trained in a way that permitted them to
ignore those data. They were smug and did not want to consider alternatives that required them to change their outlook
and practice." I do not think that smugness was a major factor
or explanation. Smugness implies contentment with outcomes.
The medical community was well aware that the outcomes of
radical mastectomy—in terms of side effects (physical and psychological) and survival rates—were not cause for enthusiasm.
It was rather that they were schooled in a way of thinking and
practicing that rendered them incapable of seriously consider-
ing alternatives. The opposition and controversy cannot be
understood in terms of an individual psychology, that is, the
personalities of individual physicians. What one has to compre-

hend is the professional education and indoctrination of these individuals into their specialties and the ways in which that education and indoctrination were mightily reinforced by the culture of the hospitals in which they became embedded once their professional training was over. We use terms like stubborness, resistance, opposition, and smugness to describe individuals— and that is appropriate if one is focusing on the psychology of an individual—but when those terms are used to characterize a particular group of individuals, our conventional psychology of individuals is woefully incomplete and inadequate. One must, at the very least, look into the institutional contexts in which they "grew up," as well as the contexts in which as individuals they do what they do.

The examples I have discussed involve the field of medicine in some way. That was not happenstance. They were prologue to my purpose of indicating a striking similarity between public and medical education. I have made it clear that I believe that our schools have been intractable to the goals of reform. In one very important respect (and there are more), medical education has been intractable to reform. To view our schools as uniquely intractable—or if that term is too extreme, I will settle here for a somewhat less harsh assessment—is in its way an unfair scapegoating of schools. It also is an obstacle to the kind of conceptual imaginativeness that should inform our understanding of institutional change.

About every decade or so a prestigious group of medical educators has published a report bemoaning the fact that the attributes of caring and compassion seem to be in short supply among physicians. In my book *Caring and Compassion in Clinical Practice* (1985), I discuss physicians in general and psychiatry in particular, clinical psychologists, teachers, and lawyers in family practice. The interested reader may wish to consult that book for a more detailed discussion of what I can only go into very briefly here. At the very least, the reader will be disabused of the thought that I am picking on physicians—that is, making the same mistake as those who pick on schools as having unique problems. These medical educators are not only reflecting their concerns. In the more recent reports they acknowledge a growing public dissatisfaction with the attitudes, styles, and practices of physicians in regard to caring and compassion. What is at issue is not whatever is subsumed under the concept of courtesy, but rather an insensitivity to the plight of sick people—their needs, wants, and complaints—that not only leaves them anxious, ambivalent, hostilely dependent, and regarding themselves as ignoramuses but also subverts preventive actions on the part of physicians and patient. In short, too many physicians pay only lip service to their obligations as healers. It is relevant to note here that since World War II the federal government and many well-heeled foundations have poured billions of dollars into medical research and training. For all practical purposes, none of it has been concerned with the ways in which physicians appropriately or inappropriately manifest caring and compassion, and with what consequences. As a research area it is nonexistent, despite the concerns of some medical educators and the dramatic increase in the number of published personal accounts (some of them best-sellers) detailing the lack of caring and compassion among physicians.

Despite the urgency of more recent reports, why has medical education been intractable to change in regard to fostering caring and compassion in students? Two points are evident in these reports. The first is the sense of concern and urgency conveyed in the message that something is very wrong, the situation is getting worse not better, and change is necessary. The second point is that the problem inheres in the culture of medical schools—that is, in their traditions, organization, and power structure. That is putting it baldly; the reports describe it more subtly, less challengingly, more allusively. However, anyone familiar with medical schools (and their associated medical centers) will have no difficulty concluding that the writers of these reports are knowledgeable about the politics and power structure of these schools. (No one with such familiarity has ever disagreed with my assertion that medical schools and centers are the last remaining jungles in American society. Certainly, no member of a medical school faculty has disagreed with that description.) Implicitly, these reports indicate that the desired change cannot occur unless there are changes in power structure, because it is that structure (and its historical development) that determines curriculum priorities—for example, how much exposure to which departments students will get. How student time is or should be allocated is the single most potent source of internecine strife in medical schools. Departmental status and power are at stake, and those with the most power put psychological attitudes, skills, and interpersonal sensitivity very low on their priority list, if on that list at all.

So what do these reports recommend? It is probably not unfair to say that they manage completely not to take seriously their implicit diagnosis and offer instead bromides and a few add-ons to the curriculum. These reports are or will be as ineffective as the scores of reports on the reform of public schools. In the case of the writers of reports for reform of public education, I have concluded that they are unfamiliar with schools. I cannot conclude that about the authors of reports on reform of medical education. They know better. Enough to know that the situation is intractable?

I am not offering a "theory" of change or a catalogue of obstacles to institutional change. I have employed these examples for two purposes. The first is to widen our horizons about what is involved in changing any educational institution—that is, to indicate that, in principle, reforming our public schools is but one instance of an educational setting that needs to change, that it is not the only educational setting that mightily affects us as individuals and a society. The second reason is to emphasize how extraordinarily difficult it is to face the fact of intractability to change and our inability to consider alternatives. To be able to consider alternatives, one must first be dissatisfied with things as they are. Dissatisfaction with public school and medical education is not hard to find, although the public is far less aware of the strength and substance of dissatisfaction with medical than with public education. In both instances, however, the dissatisfaction is not informed by the knowledge that both have been intractable to past efforts at change and will continue to be so to efforts that are based on the same faulty diagnosis. Even to consider intractability as a hypothesis requires more than dissatisfaction. It requires, in

part, confronting the failures of the past, especially their undergirding axioms—those unarticulated, not-to-be-challenged
assumptions so effectively assimilated by us in the course of
our socialization into society. Their silent nature constricts our
capacity to consider alternatives. I end this chapter with a brief
examination of one such axiom.

In my book *The Culture of the School and the Problem of Change*
(first published in 1973), I asked: Why is it so difficult to change
schools? What do we have to know to explain past failures and
to increase the chances that future efforts will succeed? I wrote
that book as an exercise in prediction—a forecast that the myriad of efforts in the sixties to reform our schools would fail.
That book was well received, especially by those who had participated in these efforts, and its prediction was confirmed by
major evaluations of those efforts that were published subse-
quently. A decade later I started to prepare a second edition
of that book (1982). Midway through the writing, I became
aware of the very unsettling fact that my thinking, like that of
everybody else, rested on an axiom that wholly or in large part
was invalid. The axiom was that education (schooling) best takes
place in encapsulated classrooms in encapsulated schools. So,
when I finished the second edition, I began to examine seriously the implications of the axiom's invalidity, and then I wrote
*Schooling in America: Scapegoat and Salvation* (1983). Very briefly,
I argued as follows:

1.  Schools generally are and have been uninteresting places
    for students and others. They are intellectually boring
    places.
2.  In this century, developments in the mass media, and their
    ever-growing influence (especially through television), have
    created for young people a wide, unbridgeable, experi-
    enced gulf between two worlds: that of the classroom and
    school and the "real" world. In terms of interest and chal-
    lenge, the former cannot hold a candle to the latter.
3.  By virtue of their encapsulation, physical and otherwise,
    schools have two virtually impossible and related tasks: to
    simulate the conditions that engender interest, challenge,

and curiosity, and to make the acquisition of knowledge and cognitive skills personally important and meaningful.

4.  As long as we uncritically accept the axiom and think of reform only in terms of altering classrooms and schools—what goes on in them—educational reform is doomed.

5.  There are alternative ways of conceiving and structuring formal education. They would require two things: recognizing the invalidity of the axiom, and the use of non-school sites for learning. In the book I give concrete examples of what can happen if we can allow ourselves to consider alternatives. Indeed, I give examples of what does and can happen when those alternatives have been taken seriously.

6.  I recognize how difficult it will be for people to consider these alternatives. It took me decades to get to the point where I could consider alternatives, and that was only possible when I confronted the intractability of schools to change.

During the week I was writing this chapter, the following column by Albert Shanker appeared in the Sunday *New York Times* for October 22, 1989. I am grateful for his permission to reprint the column.

*What's Wrong With Schools?*
### Ask The Kids

One of the most important transformations in the world of work over the past several years has been the involvement of workers in decisions about the production process. When workers were isolated on an assembly line, they just followed orders. Nobody considered asking them about the best way to do their jobs. Now, people are finding that following workers' suggestions about how to make a product can lead to big improvements in the quality of the product.

Unfortunately, the people in public education haven't yet learned to listen to the workers in our schools. It's true that teachers have gotten a chance to express their views through surveys and polls. As a result, the public now knows what they think about their work, why they remain in or quit teaching and what they think might make the schools better—even if these views haven't yet made much difference in the way schools are run. But another group of workers in our schools are ignored—just like the assembly-line workers in a factory used to be. I'm talking about the students.

We often act as though students are the products of school, when, in fact, kids must be the workers in order to learn. They must want to come to school, and they must be willing to work, even when no one is hanging over them. If we can't achieve this, no kind of school reform, however ambitious, will improve student learning and public education. So it's hard to explain why we don't routinely ask kids—especially kids in trouble—about how to improve schools.

We now have some answers in *When I Was Young I Loved School: Dropping Out and Hanging In,* a collection of 23 interviews with teenage students and former students presented by Children's Express, a news service staffed by kids. No adults were present when the teenage editors of Children's Express conducted their interviews. So we get the authentic voices of kids talking to kids about their lives, in school and out, instead of the stuff kids think adults would like to hear.

The voices are many and varied, and some of the stories are painful, but these kids aren't whiners. The ones who dropped out don't try to shift the responsibility for their actions on to the schools and their teachers—though a number do talk about the important positive difference teachers can make in keeping would-be-dropouts in school. They are also frank about the things that made school hard for them to take. And much of what they say confirms what we already know about our problems in the way our schools are organized.

Some talk about getting lost in schools that are large and impersonal. One girl, who dropped out and then dropped back in, describes how hard it was for her to make the transition from junior high school to high school: "I don't think I was ready for high school. It was really crowded and I was nervous, too." And big classes can add to the impersonality by ruling out any close contact with teachers. As another girl says, "It's not the teacher's attitude. . . . I mean, with thirty-five students in a class, how is a teacher going to notice whether a couple of students are in all of their classes." In this setup, teachers, too, are the victims.

Many of the interviews complain about being turned off by what goes on in the classroom—**boring** is the way they usually describe it. One boy who dropped out when he was a senior in high school explains that though he reads books at home, "I didn't like doing school work. . . . School was boring. And the school work I was learning was boring. Boring, boring, boring." Another boy, who has plenty of spirit and ingenuity, talks about getting **his** intellectual challenge from breaking school rules: "School was boring because you had to many classes to go to. The fun part was skipping or always doing something wrong. You always have to have some kinds of adventure in your life . . ."

A bright girl who dropped out—and who is more analytical about the way learning is organized in school—contrasts the kind of learning she enjoys with the arbitrariness and rigidity of what goes on in the classroom: "I don't really mind learning, if I'm talking with somebody and they're telling me something interesting. It's different. But . . . sitting in a classroom with this person teaching you, pointing to the blackboard, and all these people sitting behind their desks. I don't know. If there was a different way to learn or a funnier way, I'd do it in a minute."

A different way to learn is what the kids are calling for—even one of the least gifted, a youngster for whom sitting still is difficult and who confesses that what he didn't like about school was that the "classes were too long." All of them are talking about how our one-size-fits-all delivery system—which mandates that everyone learn the same thing at the same time, no matter what their individual needs—has failed them.

*When I Was Young I Loved School* is not a scientific sampling of student opinion, but the interviews speak powerfully of what it's like to feel lost and unconnected to the school culture and unconnected to what's going on in the classroom. And as we look around for ways to make schools decent workplaces for the students we'd be foolish to ignore this kind of testimony. In fact, we should hope for more.

The study Shanker refers to may not be a scientific sampling of student experience, but there have been such studies (for example, Buxton, 1973) that confirm what Shanker says.

*Schooling In America* was what is called a critical success, which means, among other things, that very few people read it. What would have occasioned surprise is if what I proposed was taken seriously in practice. I did not say what I did because I was convinced that the alternatives I was proposing were sure-fire remedies for our educational ills, or that implementing them would be other than a soul-trying process encountering a mine field of obstacles. I wrote the book as a way of saying: if one directly confronts and accepts the fact of intractability; if one concludes that the situation requires a radical change in accustomed ways of diagnosing the problem; if one can come to challenge the underlying axiom and free oneself to consider alternatives, then here is one way of thinking about alternatives for future actions. We are taught that two parallel lines will never meet in space. Someone came along who challenged that axiom and developed a new geometry, a contribution crucial to Einstein's theories and demonstrations. We are not constructed to live without axioms. We should be grateful that we are constructed to be able to challenge and change axioms when they have outlived their usefulness. It is not easy.

# 7

# REFORM EFFORTS: IMPLEMENTATION, IMITATION, AND REPLICATION

THIS CHAPTER IS ABOUT THE IMAGERY OF EDUCATIONAL REFORM, by which I mean the pictures conjured up in our minds when we think about the change process. The imagery is very similar—I would say identical—to that about medical advances. The researcher in the laboratory seeks new knowledge relevant to a disease; if he or she is successful, a basis is provided for applying the findings as a preventive for the disease or as a cure or as a diluter of its adverse consequences. The process begins with a recognized practical problem; it is redefined to allow aspects of it to be studied in the laboratory, and if the findings are positive, they are used as treatment for those who have the disease. Several questions inform the process: What do we know about the disease? How and to what extent can aspects of it be simulated in the laboratory? What are the dangers of or obstacles to using findings for treatment? That last question is recognition that the process starts because there are unknowns about the disease; if there were no unknowns, there would be no need for the research. The process can be put in another way. You start with how well you understand the disease in its naturally occurring context; you seek to understand your lab-

**117**

oratory findings in that context; and you then seek ways to justify connecting those two kinds of understanding. Far more often than not, making those connections enlarges understanding of both the naturally occurring and laboratory contexts.

No less than in medicine, many efforts at educational reform are justified on the basis of research studies. So, for example, the massive curriculum changes that were initiated in the sixties were justified on the basis of research studies that demonstrated that the new curricula (and its associated features) had significantly more desirable educational outcomes than those previously used. If these studies were not experimental in methodology (for example, no comparison groups, no before or after measures, no "hard" data), it said less about the researchers' devotion to the canons of science and the rules of evidence than it did about what one is realistically up against in conducting research in education. In this respect, the imagery of white-coated researchers working in instrument-filled, encapsulated laboratories does not hold for the curriculum researchers. Nevertheless, they presented their findings as the fruits of efforts demonstrating that customary practice in the naturally occurring school context was inferior to the practice they had employed in their equivalent of a research laboratory. It is not unduly pushing the analogy to the medical laboratory to say that they proceeded as if they understood a great deal about a particular disease in schools as well as they understood what they had done in their "labs." Connecting the two was presumably a technical problem—that is, the logistical process of substituting a new curriculum for the old one. The basic understandings of the two contexts had been achieved, at least to the degree justifying action. Why, then, did their efforts end up as disasters? Before dealing with that question, let us look a bit more closely at medical research.

The history of medical research has glorious and inglorious features. No less than in educational research, there have been in medical research fads and fashions of which many people have been victims. The reasons are many, but prominent among them has been the failure of researchers to ask and adequately answer the three questions: How well do I understand the disease in its naturally occurring context? How well have I simulated aspects of it in my laboratory? What are the pitfalls that I may encounter if I use my findings for treatment in light of the unknowns in the naturally occurring context? It was the failure to deal seriously with these questions that over time sensitized the medical community and the general public to the moral dimensions of medical research. It was not enough to cloak one's efforts in the garments of science as an excuse for sloppy thinking or for adverse and sometimes lethal side effects. It is praiseworthy to seek new knowledge, to seek to cure or ameliorate or prevent disease, but in that seeking you have the responsibility not to overestimate your understanding of what and whom you seek to affect. That is putting it negatively. It would be better to say that the responsibility requires that your first obligation, scientific and moral, is to understand the nature of the organism in as many of its aspects as are considered relevant to the disease. You start and end there.

Why is it that, today in medicine, laboratory-derived knowledge cannot be applied without satisfying numerous formal and legal hurdles? And there are some who say that the number of those hurdles is too few and their quality or rigor too low. (The same situation and argument hold for the use of chemical ingredients in foods.) The answer is that in the past there were too many scandalous examples of researchers who confused what they thought was a good idea with good practice—that is, they flew into action, overestimating what they knew and heedless of its consequences for those they sought to help. These were examples, it needs to be emphasized, of poor science and of moral insensitivity. The hurdles were erected to protect science and the public. Do you know enough about the "real life" context to justify being permitted to intervene? Put another way, how well did you understand that context and how well do you understand it now? From what and to what are you extrapolating? I am not here referring to examples of blatant moral insensitivity—for example, treating one group of Blacks with an anti-syphilitic drug and doing nothing for a "control" group of Blacks. I am referring to examples in which the moral insensitivity is more than matched by poor science.

The history of educational reform, like that of medicine, is replete with examples of interventions that either failed or had adverse effects because those involved had only the most superficial and distorted conception of the culture of the schools they were supposed to change. This is not to say that all of these interventions were stimulated by "bad" ideas. That is not the case. Nor is it the case that those justifying the interventions were morally delinquent. There is a difference between ignorance and moral insensitivity, although in its consequences ignorance can bring the moral issue to the fore. But if these failures demonstrate anything, it is how ignorant the interveners were about the "host organism" they sought to improve. Let me give one illustration from today's scene.

At a convention symposium, the head of a state bureau was describing an experimental program to place in schools certain health and social services the aim of which would be to make these services available to parents and children more quickly and effectively. These services were to be in the schools but not administratively responsible to them. It was assumed that by having the services in the schools, and not here and there in the community, coordination and collaboration between schools and services would occur. Three sites had been chosen: one urban, one suburban, and one rural. Schools in the state had been apprised of the program and invited to apply.

This program did not come from nowhere but was a direct result of a much described and discussed effort, presumably successful, in another state. It was a good idea for which there seemed to be evidence that it worked. If that evidence was soft and anecdotal, the fact remains that it was used as a basis for the program this bureau chief was spearheading. It was and is a good idea, as any teacher or administrator dealing with problem children and families will attest. That the road to hell is paved with good ideas and intentions seems never to have occurred to this spearheader.

He began his presentation by humorously relating his experience several days earlier in his meetings with parents from the three chosen schools. Apparently, there were many parents who did not look kindly on the program, although he did not say why. He went on to describe the program and why it would be a boon to everyone. After his presentation I asked the following questions, to which I received short replies:

1. How well was he replicating the conditions and the step-by-step process that characterized the program in the other state? His answer was unrevealing, leading me (and others) to conclude that this was no replication, or an approximation of one.

2. In light of what he had indicated about parental response, was he saying that parents had not been involved in the decision to enter the program? Yes, he reluctantly said, that was the case.

3. Was it the case that the decision to participate was made by the superintendent (with the approval of the board of education) and that teachers had not been consulted, informally or formally? Yes, that was the case.

4. Since the new services would require space, and space is usually at a premium, was it not likely that teachers and others would not take kindly to either giving up space or using it for purposes other than those to which they had given a higher priority? He had never thought of that.

5. Because the health and social service personnel who would now be in the schools were unfamiliar with schools, what had been planned to alert them to the nature of the school culture? Nothing.

6. What problems would predictably arise between these new professionals and those "indigenous" to schools in light of the fact that the former would be administratively autonomous? In asking that question, I made it clear that I was not necessarily suggesting that they not be autonomous or that there were no other alternatives. His answer was that with good will, and a desire to help children, the problems would not be serious.

I wanted to ask more questions, but it was not seemly to hog the discussion. After the symposium, however, two people who had direct knowledge of the three school sites came up to tell me that the problems addressed by my questions were only the tip of the iceberg. The point of the anecdote is not to show that the program director was a poor implementer but rather that he was ignorant of the culture of schools and school systems, no less so than the superintendents who made the decision to participate. What they had in common was the imagery associated with the phrase "delivery of services": there are services, there are people who need them, and you deliver the services the way mail is delivered. It is so easy to diagram! So efficient! So self-defeating.

There are two kinds of basic understandings or problems that should inform implementation. The first is what may be loosely termed theoretical: the weaving of a conceptual framework that makes sense of your ideas—that is, their interrelationships, the "real world" context from which they arose, their connections with the ideas and efforts of others, the different weights you assign to this or that factor. It is a framework in the present that has a past and a future direction. The second basic problem is: since you are developing the framework because it has relevance for human behavior, you seek to understand and change in a particular social-institutional context. How well do you understand that context? That context has structure, implicit and explicit rules, traditions, power relationships, and purposes variously defined by its members. It is dynamic in that it is characterized by continuous activity and interchanges both within its boundaries and between it and its community surround. It is a context that can be described, but it is not a context that can be understood by what we ordinarily mean by description. It has covert as well as overt features.

These two basic problems or understandings are not independent of each other. Each is actually within the other. The weaver of the conceptual framework is at the same time the "knower" of the context. Unfortunately, too many times the weaver of the framework is unaware how inadequately he knows the context. He or she assumes a degree of understanding the limits of which only become clear when implementation fails. They do not know the territory, although they have worked in it for a long time.

Theory is a necessary myth that we construct to understand something we know we understand incompletely. Theory is a deliberate attempt to go beyond what we know or to correct what we think are the erroneous explanations of others. It is intended to make a difference not only on the level of theory but on the level of action, be it in a laboratory, a classroom, or a school. It is a statement that says: if you think about the problems in this way, and you do such and such, you will observe something the theory predicts that was not predictable before. Theory is supposed to change our perception of phenomena in a certain context, and that change requires actions consistent with that change. Educational reform rarely derives from whatever we mean by theory but rather from opinion, anecdote, an uncritical acceptance of research, or a desperation. I do not say this unkindly. We do and should feel compelled to act when it is obvious that our schools are not accomplishing what we desire. One does not sit back and wait until unalloyed wisdom or the truth appears somehow, somewhere on the scene. If anything is understandable, it is the feeling of reformers that something needs to be done. My quarrel with reformers is twofold. The first is their inability or reluctance to face up to the intractability of schools to past efforts of reform. The second, more central to this chapter, is the failure to recognize that they do have an implicit theory about how to achieve change: change can come about by proclaiming new policies, or by legislation, or by new performance standards, or by creating a shape-up-or-ship-out ambience, or all of the preceding. It is a conception that in principle is similar to how you go about creating and improving an assembly line—that is, what it means to those who work on the assembly line is of secondary significance, if it has any significance at all. The workers (read: educational personnel) *will* change. It is a theory that assumes an understanding of schools as erroneous as it is laughable—not funny laughable, but grimly laughable.

One more example. As indicated earlier in this book, there

are a few places where the running of schools has been given to teachers, parents, and representatives of other community groups having a vested interest in schools. These are interesting and serious experiments to alter power relationships and loci of responsibility. They have received a good deal of attention, but few takers elsewhere. As best as I can determine, these efforts were initiated by leaders with a refreshingly comprehensive understanding of the school culture, a willingness to take risks, and a resolve to do more than proclaim a new policy.[1] How things will work we do not know, and it is unlikely that these efforts will be comprehensively described and evaluated so as to permit secure conclusions. But the point here is that I have been able to observe, although far from comprehensively, two instances where superintendents are seeking to imitate these innovative efforts. If they are not horror stories, neither do they disconfirm the adage that the more things change the more they remain the same. In neither instance did the superintendent make the effort to determine why and how the efforts he seeks to imitate came about: the role of leadership, the resistances encountered and the degree to which they were overcome, the appearances versus the realities (there is always a discrepancy), the intended and unintended consequences, and so on. This is why I used the verb *imitate* and not *replicate*. What is going on is sloganeering and advertising, imitation of surface phenomena devoid of substance. Replication suggests a degree of comprehension that imitation does not capture. These are instances of what someone called the "replication of nonevents."

Here is a final example. Many have heard about the New York industrialist, Mr. Lang, who was invited to address the graduating students at a ghetto elementary school. (If my memory is correct, it was the school that Lang had attended as a child.) Sitting on the podium looking down on the Black and Hispanic students and parents, Lang concluded that what he had intended to say was the kind of bromide the audience did not need. Instead, Lang told the students: if you proceed through the grades and are graduated from high school, I will underwrite your college education. What has happened to these students and families has not been systematically described. Occasionally, there are stories in the mass media describing Lang's commendable degree of personal commitment and involvement in the lives and career paths of these students. Apparently—and I say apparently because there are no published data—the educational outcomes have been remarkable. I have no trouble accepting these outcomes on faith, but I also have no basis for saying that I understand how they have been achieved. That Lang gave these students and families a basis for reaching to the future is obvious, but no one, I assume, would say that providing that basis is an explanation. Indeed, from the published anecdotes it is clear that a lot more went on and was done with the students and their families than the dangling of a financial reward. So, if you accept the outcomes as I do, you also have to accept that we have no basis for saying that we know what a replication should require. This is crucial in two related ways: the effort is potentially very important, so important that if replications should turn out to be far less successful, or even failures, we would not know what to conclude except that here is another example of a good idea that is not so good.

From what we know of the effort, Lang has an implicit theory of change consisting of at least five assumptions. The first is that an outside agent for change is necessary—that is, the change will not or cannot come about from within. Second, the change must involve parents and community resources. Third, sustaining motivation in students and families demands that one enter their lives in whatever ways are necessary in and out of school. Fourth, the outside force for change inevitably alters existing attitudes and power relationships because those alterations come to be seen as "friendly" to diverse vested interests. Fifth, students should experience less discontinuity (personal, educational, and social) between the school and nonschool worlds.

Lang does not purport to be an educational theorist and he may not even agree with what I have described as his implicit theory. But, I would argue, the changes he initiated are inexplicable without those five assumptions. There is really a sixth assumption: whoever initiates such an effort has to commit himself or herself to a tremendously time-consuming and personally demanding degree. When Lang took groups of students in his car to see college campuses, to begin to understand what college may mean, to give substance to fantasies about what life can have in store for them—*that* is commitment. If Lang is no theorist, neither is he a scientist and therefore he cannot ask: was there anything special about that elementary school—its students, parents, principal (who invited him), and staff—before Lang appeared on the scene? If this was not the modal ghetto school, we ought (we need) to know that for purposes of replication. If it did have special characteristics, this in no way detracts from what Lang has done. But it would tell us something very important about the conditions that facilitate change, or make it possible. Lang formed a foundation for the purpose of stimulating other affluent people to adopt a school and to provide assistance. It is the "I Have a Dream Foundation." And now for my experience with an effort that foundation has sponsored.

I was visiting a colleague in a midwestern state whose research involved a number of inner-city schools. His research had received play in the newspapers, as a result of which he received a telephone call from an affluent couple who two years before had adopted the sixth-grade students of an inner-city school in a nearby city, in conjunction with Lang's foundation. Would my friend meet with them to explore whether his program was applicable to their efforts? Of course, he said yes. The meeting was to take place on the day of my visit. My friend asked if I could attend and they agreed. It was not an easy meeting, despite the fact that this was as attractive, bright, and well-intentioned (and relatively young) a couple as one could meet. Here, in brief, are the contents of the meeting:

1.  My friend and the couple agreed that what he was doing was quite applicable to their efforts. But my friend said that for him to justify participation (that is, in terms of his research program) would require at least a partial evaluation of what was being done. To this the couple replied

that Lang, and therefore they, were opposed to formal evaluations.

2. They had hired a director who was at our meeting, a minority person familiar with schools. He had makeshift offices in the two middle schools to which the sixth graders had gone. Both were problem-laden schools, one far more than the other. In terms of time, energy, and involvement, this couple were miles from Lang. They were concerned, they tried to know what was going on, but they were not involved in the lives of other than a few students, and not in the lives of families most of whom lived in a troubled housing project.

3. There were teachers and administrators in the middle school who resented the special attention the cohort received while other students received none. In fact, there was a tendency for the school staff mechanically to refer cohort children with problems to the director. The director made it clear that the two middle schools were not all that enthusiastic about the program. He also made it clear that he felt himself to be in a very difficult role: in the school but not of it.

4. By the end of the sixth grade, before going to the middle schools, a large percentage of the cohort was below, some very much below, grade level in achievement. This was making classroom life for them difficult and unrewarding. Remedial and enrichment experiences were developed for them outside of school, but the director did not feel that this was engendering increased motivation or achievement.

5. My friend and I concluded that little effort, and that unimaginative, had gone into securing parental involvement or commitment. Almost all the families lived in a housing project, but there were no ongoing activities there related to the program. The director and the couple seemed perplexed about what they should do and how to do it.

Of two things my friend and I were certain: the director and the couple were unhappy with what was going on, and the program was floundering to failure. Some of the students will undoubtedly benefit from the program. I would be surprised if that were true for more than a few. But that is not my point here. This effort is clearly not a replication of Lang's initial program, keeping in mind that we really know pitifully little about the program—certainly not enough to say what a replication should be.

As a postscript, I received a letter from my friend that contained the following:

> Several weeks after that first meeting, I asked to meet with them again. I did this hesitantly but, like you, I felt much was at stake, i.e., much more than this particular effort. When we met I made this pitch: in light of what they had described, a formal evaluation could be very productive *for the program.* I told them about two of my school experiences where I spent upward of a year carrying out studies which did not pan out. But I learned a great deal that required me to think and act differently in subsequent years, with far more success in these intervention studies. The director seemed willing, the husband was on the fence, but the wife was opposed. My puzzlement must have registered on my face because after a long awkward silence she said: "We have put a lot of money into this project. Over the next six or seven years we will have given it our time, energy, and devotion. If this should turn out to be a failure, how would I feel? I do not want to face that. I would rather not."

I am partisan of the view that to understand all is to forgive all, but there are limits beyond which you have to pass judgment. What the wife said is completely understandable to me and not foreign to my personal experience. But when your understanding is about something that involves more than you as an individual—that is, the present and future of others—then refraining from judgment, or from saying that not judging is irresponsible or even morally wrong, would be like compounding a felony. To own up to failure is as necessary as it is tormenting. That is why in this book I have focused on the inability of educational reformers to confront intractability. The imagery of educational reform says more about hope and good intentions than it does about anything else. That the road to hell is indeed paved with good intentions is an adage quite appropriate to the history of educational reform.

I am told by a friend who is acquainted with two other couples sponsoring programs like Lang's that what I have related here holds for their efforts as well. I should also note that my counterintelligence indicates that the Chicago public school created, developed, and financed by Chicago industrialists is, despite the national publicity it has received, very unlikely to achieve its goals. My information here is not gossip. I mention it to make the point that, in their own companies, these business executives would never (perhaps too strong a word) undertake a major reform that they did not sedulously monitor, evaluate, and report. Publicity is not evaluation. No less than in the private sector, there are bottom-line criteria for judging whether an educational reform is achieving its stated purposes. As in the Lang programs, there is reason to believe that the Chicago instance is not being carefully, even semi-dispassionately, logged and evaluated. How do you build into a new school self-correcting forums and mechanisms so absent in our schools? Put that way, the task is not evaluation in the narrow sense but development of an organizational culture that makes self-correction a norm and not a war.

What I have said in this chapter was not for the purpose of celebrating the importance of research or evaluation. We have had a surfeit of educational research (and evaluation of non-events) that is subject to the criticism of being informed by a most superficial comprehension of the contexts in which educational problems or phenomena arise. In itself that is no cause for worry. It is when the conclusions of research become the basis of action in seemingly similar contexts that the powering imagery is illuminated: you *apply* the conclusions, you *deliver* the knowledge, you *perform* the operation as if the object of it is a passive, anesthetized patient. It is a problem in application only if it derives from and rests on how well you have answered a prior basic question: how well do you understand the culture of the context in which the problem arose and in which you seek to intervene? Our inadequate answers to that question explain a good deal about the failures of educational reform. And that is true for most of the educational research community as well as for those nonresearchers who have, as they should, grappled with reform.

I end this chapter with one of the few exceptions to what I have said. In 1966 I invited Emory Cowen of the University of Rochester to come to the Yale Psycho-Educational Clinic to tell us about his research in the Rochester elementary schools. The aim of his project was to devise means to identify problem children and to provide them a remedial service *in the schools,* a service that would be practical and preventive. Two things were remarkable in his presentation. The first was his long-term goal of developing a program that not only could be scientifically justified in terms of data and reporting but also could be demonstrated to be applicable to any elementary school. That is to say, it was not his goal only to demonstrate that the program would be beneficial for students in the few schools in which he was working, or that having presented his findings he would then expect that those who read his publications would seek to apply their contents. On the contrary, he was quite sensitive to the pitfalls of replication and hoped ultimately to create a training center for those who wanted to apply his program. But that was a long way off. The point here is that Cowen, who had already spent nearly a decade in this research, was committing his future to the program, not only to collect data but also to figure out how the program could be disseminated in a way consistent with its purposes and procedures. If Cowen is a very modest person, his goals were otherwise.

The second remarkable feature of his presentation—occupying half of the meeting—was his detailed (and uproarious) account of all the mistakes he had made that illustrated his lack of understanding of schools, especially concerning issues of status and power—for example, his relationship with diverse school personnel; the relationship between teachers and Cowen's helping, nonprofessional aides; and the relationships between a school and "downtown." Cowen was a very fast learner from failure.

Anyone who reads the scores of research publications of Cowen and his colleagues will have great difficulty downplaying the significance of what he has done. Through more than three decades, he and his students have personally trained scores of representatives from schools around the country. They have received national funding which, together with their personal and successful efforts to get state legislatures to budget in these programs, has had more than a minor impact.[2] If Cowen has devoted his professional life to the project, it is not only because his data are so clear and compelling but also because he knows the difference between imitation and replication. This brings me to Roger Weissberg, Cowen's student and colleague, who joined the Yale faculty seven years ago.

When Weissberg came to Yale, he told me about his research program in social problem solving in school children. He had devised ways of influencing children's social problem skills, in its way a lineal descendant of Cowen's primary prevention project. His goal was to gain entry into the New Haven schools and ultimately to have his program in most, if not all, of that system. At the same time, he aimed at getting the state legislature to fund schools desiring to use Cowen's program. Again, if Weissberg is a modest individual, his goals were not. He asked if I had any advice in regard to people with whom he should talk. I was of two minds. I wanted to say, and did say with laughter, that anyone who willingly sought to be involved in the New Haven school system must have a deep reservoir of masochistic needs. And yet, the very fact that he had asked me whom to talk to indicated that he understood the difference between formal and informal power. I can honestly say that Weissberg went about the port-of-entry problem in as sophisticated and successful a way as I have ever witnessed. He does have an unplumbed reservoir of patience. He understands the importance of constituency building. He understands the culture of schools, especially in regard to its power relationships and dynamics. And he knows the difference between compromise and corruption in regard to goals. I am not describing a paragon of virtues and wisdom but someone who today is spearheading an effort at a degree of system-wide curriculum change that I had thought unrealistic, if only because the system had heretofore been intractable to any meaningful change. But I did not then really know Roger Weissberg. I did not know that this young man had such a basic understanding of the school culture—something I should have known, given who his mentor was.

Cowen and Weissberg are among the few who know what they are up against in changing any aspect of a school or school system. What these few have understood is that good ideas and good intentions are not enough, and that replication and imitation are not the same. No one more than I respects the contributions of John Dewey to our understanding of human behavior generally and education in particular. But in one respect, he was grievously in error. What Dewey created, learned, and sustained in his lab school at the University of Chicago will be an important chapter in the history of education. He set up that school for many reasons, not the least of which derived from his observations of what children were subjected to in classrooms. Dewey's writing style was not what one would call passionate, but when he described and discussed the public school classroom, his sense of outrage came through. Dewey intended his lab school to be not only a test and demonstration of his ideas but also the basis for changing schools. He devoted a lot of time and energy disseminating his theories, findings, and accomplishments. The lab school became a center of national interest. But Dewey was oblivious to two problems. The first was that creating a lab school under favorable conditions (relatively speaking) was by no means the same as changing an existing school or school system. The second was that in focusing his attention on the encapsulated classroom, Dewey was ignoring or oblivious to the culture of schools and school systems and, therefore, to the predictable problems the change process engenders. It is not surprising that what Dewey did was imitated not replicated, a fact that he came to appreciate. But, it could be argued, how many other Deweys are there? How often do the conditions favorable to either creation or change obtain? The answer to the first question is none, and the answer to the second is very seldom. If in this century there has been only one Dewey, and if favorable conditions for creation and change are rare, do we call it a day? Of course not. Unless you enjoy wallowing in despair, railing against a world inhospitable to your ends, unwilling or unable to commit yourself to what you believe in, retreating as if you have learned nothing and there are no truths, allergic to approximations that fall far short of perfection, there is no alternative to taking a stand. From a purely personal as well as a societal perspective, there is too much at stake. To live in perilous times is no warrant for imperiling your integrity.

### Notes

1. One of the best and most stirring accounts of what can happen when an educational leader, in this case a principal, undertakes to change a school is Kammeraad-Campbell's *Doc. The Story of Dennis Littky and His Fight for a Better School* (1989). I know Littky, who is atypical in several respects: his understanding of the culture of schools and its accustomed pattern of power relationships, his grasp of what makes learning interesting and productive for students and teachers, his knowledge of and relationship to diverse community groups, and his courage to fight what he considers to be the good fight, being always mindful that without supportive constituencies the fight will be short and futile. In brief, he not only understands schools but also communities. For him schools should not be walled off from their community surround. What is atypical about him is less his courage than his willingness to confront those factors that have made schools intractable to change. The book describes what happened in a small, poor, conservative New Hampshire town. What it does not describe is what Littky had earlier done in an affluent Long Island community, albeit with less open warfare.

2. The interested reader should consult E. L. Cowen and others, "State-Level Dissemination of a Program for Early

Detection and Prevention of School Maladjustment," *Professional Psychology: Research and Practice,* 1989, *20* (5), 309–314. The bibliography in that article lists earlier publications describing the work of Cowen and his colleagues.

# 8

# FOR WHOM DO SCHOOLS EXIST?

WE CAN CHANGE POWER RELATIONSHIPS, CURRICULA, STANDARDS, the organization of the school day, the preparation and credentialing of school personnel, and the criteria for promotion and graduation. But to what ends? What are the aims of schools? The teacher in front of a class of students has not only immediate aims but also ones that are near and far term. I shall assume that no one would say that it is sufficient that a teacher's aims over the school year concern only the acquisition of information and technical skills. These aims are certainly important, but if we do not accept them as sufficient, it is because we intuitively feel that there is a difference between information and knowledge, just as we should not confuse facts with the truth. When the term "carnal knowledge" is used in the Bible, it does not refer to the facts or processes of sexual intercourse but to a comprehension that goes far beyond the factual, frequently in the context of morality and intrapsychic conflict. That is to say, the "know" in knowledge is not derivable only from the facts. There is, you might say, "know" knowledge and fact knowledge. To "understand" facts literally means to grasp what is "under" them: a context of meanings and re-

lationships. I have never met anyone who denied the importance of that kind of understanding, regardless of how widely
we differed on other educational issues. No one is comfortable
with the imagery of children as fact machines. We want more
for them, and if schools are generally uninteresting places to
children, it is because they want more but rarely get it.

I must here avoid a trap into which almost all educational
reformers have fallen. Indeed, it is no less the case for the
public generally. I refer to the assumption, indeed it is one of
those unverbalized axioms, that schools do and should exist
primarily for students, that is, the aims of education are the
aims we have for our children. If questioning that assumption
seems strange, it is testimony to the strength of what is now a
self-defeating tradition. Let me, therefore, explain how I came
to question the tradition.

In the early sixties I directed the Yale Psycho-Educational
Clinic, which was not a clinic in the usual sense that people
could refer themselves for our services. We worked *in* classrooms and in nonschool settings that were nevertheless educational in their purposes. One of the reasons that clinic was
started is wrapped up in the question: why do so many old and
new settings fail of their purposes? And by *fail* I mean two
things: they go out of existence, or they continue to survive
even though they are not achieving their stated goals. It was
not that they were not helping some people but rather that
they were quite aware of the gulf between goals and performance. Those were the days when the term *burnout* gained
currency as a way of accounting for poor staff morale, increase
in staff turnover, or the fact that people were simply giving up
and leaving the field. It is no less true today in education and
the human services generally. Burnout is a complicated phenomenon that does not have a simple explanation. But there
was one aspect of burnout and agency failure that I did think
I understood and that had to be a major part of an explanation. That aspect was another one of those axioms: the setting
exists primarily to serve others. *That* is its justification for existence. "We are judged and we judge ourselves by how well
we further growth in others who seek our help" encapsulates

the axiom. In almost all instances I have studied, that axiom undergirded settings from their creation.[1]

Here is an example. If you, as I have, ask teachers (for example, in an elementary school) how they justify the existence of their school, the answer you get is that schools exist to further the intellectual and social development of students. Now, if you ask faculty members of a university how they justify the existence of the university, in one or another way the answer is that the university primarily exists to create and sustain those conditions that enable its faculty to learn, change, and grow. (You can have a university with few or no students.) The assumption is that if those conditions exist for faculty, it increases the chances that the faculty can create and sustain those conditions for students.

The two answers are polar opposites. The public school exists for students. Period. The university exists primarily for its faculty. Stated so baldly, that latter answer will strike some people as self-serving, narcissistic, or even antisocial. The imagery of university faculty paid to investigate the problems that interest *them,* to support them in their endeavors to contribute to knowledge in ways *they* choose, does not sit well with most people. The university, of course, does not publicly proclaim that its primary justification for existence is in furthering the development of its faculty, although in its most important internal forums for discussion that justification is taken for granted. What the university does proclaim is that creating and sustaining the development of faculty makes it possible for them to create that ambience for students. At the very least, the university exists equally for faculty and students.

I am aware that colleges and universities differ dramatically in their assignment of weights in this regard. What are by conventional criteria considered our "best" colleges and universities are those that have assigned equal importance to the development of both faculty and students. There are, unfortunately, many colleges and universities that give only lip service to the needs of their faculties and consider themselves "only" teaching institutions: they, like our public schools, regard the education of students as by far their most important function.

In the scores of times I have visited such settings, I could count on hearing two things from their faculties: an expression of disappointment at the unwillingness or inability of the setting to support faculty development, and a recounting of the ways in which burdensome teaching loads and other duties over time erode satisfaction from teaching. In no less than our public schools the teachers have come to see that if conditions for their growth do not obtain, they cannot create and sustain them for students. And as in our public schools there were always a few faculty who managed somehow to keep their intellectual fires burning despite a nonsupportive institutional tradition. The fires in others had long been extinguished. In my opinion, it is extreme snobbery to judge these people as having second-rate intellects, as if institutional tradition and atmosphere have been insignificant variables in their lives. If these settings of lesser quality are impoverishing both for faculty and students, part (and only part) of the reason is the hold on the public's mind of the axioms that educational settings exist only or primarily for students, and that one can create the conditions for productive learning in students even though they do not exist for their teachers. Lest I be misunderstood: I am not saying that if, by a strange set of circumstances (the stuff of fantasy), educational settings were to accept the invalidity of the axioms and redress the imbalance, educational bliss would ensue. I am suggesting that redressing the balance increases the chances that more teachers and students will experience the sense of growth, without which life is a pointless bore.

Take the matter of sabbaticals. In our conventionally regarded "best" universities, sabbaticals are accorded to tenured faculty as a matter of course. Every seven years a faculty member may take a sabbatical at full pay for one semester or a full year at half pay. (At Yale you can take a semester off at full pay every three years.) The purposes of the sabbatical are twofold and interrelated: to free the person from all teaching and administrative responsibilities and to encourage him or her to review past accomplishments, or to take stock, or to move in new directions, or to go somewhere to learn something new. It is intended to facilitate the recharging of one's mental and personal batteries—an opportunity to get out of a rut. It is explicit that sabbaticals be used to expand one's horizons in some way. The sabbatical is not a gift from the university. It is recognition that there has to be a time when you can take distance from your accustomed routine so that when you return there will be an infusion of new energy and new ideas. I am aware that there are people who use the sabbatical to do more of what they have been doing—that is, to have more time to complete a research or scholarly endeavor. Even so, it is testimony to the obligation of the university to create conditions that are intellectually productive. More often than not, however, the sabbatical is used for acquiring new experience and new directions.

But why is the sabbatical a matter of course in relatively few colleges and universities? The usual answer is that only a few universities have the financial resources to underwrite sabbaticals. Although this is true, it hides the fact that the tradition of the sabbatical was never built into most colleges and universities because they were regarded (that is, created) as teaching institutions, just as public schools were and are. As teaching institutions, their justification was in the education of students, not in the development of their teachers. My guess is that, if presented with a rationale for the necessity of the sabbatical in teaching institutions, the founders and sustainers of these institutions would have responded with staring disbelief. If one were to present that rationale to those heading these institutions today, I doubt that more than a few would comprehend its wisdom. Certainly, most of their faculty would comprehend and agree with that rationale, and not because they confuse a sabbatical with a vacation. They know their batteries are running low.

If only on this level of rhetoric, the sabbatical has an accepted, indeed treasured, place in higher education that is clearly not the case in our public schools. If my experience is any guide, the bulk of school systems make no provision whatsoever for sabbaticals. Some make it available to one or two teachers (and some of them require a financial sacrifice on the part of the teacher). It is discouraging that the significance and necessity of sabbaticals has never been a matter for discussion by educational reformers, either those inside or outside of our schools. This silence forces me to conclude that teaching is regarded as something you can do (and do well!) day in and day out, month in and month out, year in and year out without any decrease in motivation or change in style, satisfaction, patience, sensitivity, and sense of challenge. And this can apparently be done by all teachers regardless of where they teach, what they teach, and whom they teach. It should make no difference if the teacher does not experience any collegiality, has no role in decision making, is expected to be all things to all students, and regards him or herself as a member of the educational proletariat. I do not know of any set of expectations more invalid and defeating of the aims of reform. I do not say this because I believe sabbaticals should be at the top of any list of foci for reform, but because the silence about sabbaticals says a great deal about insensitivity to how the structure and culture of schools have the effect over time of subtly but powerfully undercutting the motivation, creativity, and professional-intellectual growth of educational personnel.

Sabbaticals are not vacations in that their purpose is not to "get away from it all" but rather to get a new perspective on "it all." There are few roles as demanding of one's energy, ingenuity, sensitivity, and patience as that of the classroom teacher. I have been in hundreds of classrooms and have interviewed even more teachers for one or another research purpose. It took me years to begin to understand why the majority of teachers seem to fall short of the criteria for what I consider a teacher should be. This is not to say that most were incompetent, although some were, but rather that they had settled into a routine that guaranteed that the classroom atmosphere would lack sparkle, buoyancy, challenge, and humor. These classrooms struck me as joyless, grim affairs, certainly for students and even for most teachers. Like that of most people, including educational reformers, my explanation (early on) gave prominent place to the quality of the minds of teachers—that is, generally speaking and by conventional test criteria, they were not as bright as those in other professions, such as law, medicine, or engineering. Therefore, a top priority for educational reform was to attract to teaching more bright people. This assignment of priority rested on two assumptions. The first was that by attracting those with higher test scores, one would be getting people who had a better and broader grasp of subject matter, if only because they were more likely to be found in colleges and universities that were more intellectually demanding than teachers' colleges. The second assumption was that there was a very high correlation between intelligence and achievement test scores, on the one hand, and creativity or imaginativeness, on the other hand.

Three things required a change in my thinking. The first stemmed from a sustained and intensive immersion in a teacher preparation program in a college that had only recently been changed from a teacher-training institution to a liberal arts one. More specifically, the immersion was in an undergraduate program that prepared special education teachers. The opportunity to participate was given to me by Burton Blatt, who chaired that small department and who is one of the most unusual people I have ever known. It was through him that I learned about teacher preparation programs and began to understand how suffocating these programs could be for those seeking to become teachers. It was as if these students were adult children with no minds of their own, requiring that they be programmed like computers for their future role. However, if by conventional test criteria they were as a group unimpressive, they had the insight or maturity to conclude that their preparation was a very uninteresting, boring affair. (Indeed, one of the very few research findings in education that has withstood the test of replication is that most teachers judge their preparation to have been inadequate and irrelevant.)

The second experience that required a change in my thinking began in the early sixties, when the leadership of the New Haven schools made a valiant and successful effort to attract to teaching recent graduates from our "best" liberal arts colleges and universities. Attracting them was not very difficult because colleges campuses had many students eager to make a difference in those socially turbulent times. It was possible for those who wanted to become teachers to enroll in the summer in a teacher-training program, following which they became classroom teachers, taking a course or two during the school year. It was not unusual, given that teachers were in short supply, that some started to teach without any formal preparation. One of the things the Yale Psycho-Educational Clinic did was to initiate weekly seminars for these new teachers, the main purpose of which was to provide a forum where they could openly present and discuss whatever problems they were encountering.[2]

These new teachers were generally bright, lively, and engaged (especially in the early months in their new role). By the end of the year, one fact and one observation proved noteworthy. The fact noted was that the school systems provided no forums within the school and the system that in any way were regarded by these teachers as helpful. Each was essentially alone with his or her problems. The observation concerned the steady decline in morale among these teachers as they experienced their classrooms and their schools. The more they became aware of problems—their and their students—the more overwhelmed they became and the more they reluctantly lowered their sights. Although their energy level did not suffer, they found themselves seeking ways to defend themselves against passivity, bitterness, and an eroding sense of mission. I should note that these observations derived not only from the seminars but from our involvement in classrooms in several of the city's schools. They were not my observations alone but those of the score of clinic personnel who also were in classrooms and schools. And, it must be emphasized, these observations were no less true for new teachers who had completed an undergraduate teacher-training program in the local state college. In terms of culture shock, it made no difference where they had gone to college. It needs also to be said that those who lacked formal preparation did no worse or better than those who had such preparation. By the end of their first year, the soil I call the culture of the school had begun to sprout the weeds of burnout.[3] There were exceptions as always, but they were rare. I do not want to convey the impression that these new teachers had become wrecks or that they needed the services of psychotherapists. My message is contained in what one teacher said to me at the end of that first year: "I keep asking myself if I really want to be a teacher. Do I want to be alone all day with students who have scads of problems for which I have neither the time or knowledge? I am not blaming the kids, although some are impossible to reach or motivate, but, I keep asking myself, is this the way I will feel as the years go on? I feel so alone." What she said explains why in our book (Sarason and others, 1966), Murray Levine wrote a chapter titled "Teaching Is a Lonely Profession", which endeared us to many teachers who did not know us but who wrote to us.

During the sixties there were thousands of people from liberal arts colleges and universities who became "instant" teachers. I am not aware of any study that sought to determine what became of these people. Crucial here is how many left teaching and why? My observations, obviously based on limited experience, suggest that, on a percentage basis, more of them left teaching than was the case for those who had the usual formal preparation. We have statistics galore on many matters, important and not, concerning education. We have relatively few studies on what teaching in our schools does to teachers and other personnel. And what we have does not paint a favorable picture. Just as educational reformers have made recommendations about what they think can be done, not what needs to be done, those in the research community study what they can "measure," not what needs to be understood. There are exceptions, I know, but that is precisely what they are: exceptions. They are read but unheeded.

The third reason requiring me to alter my thinking goes back several decades to when I started a long-term research project in three very different school systems. I have to tell the reader that my formal training and experience were in clinical psychology. I mention that because training in any clinical profession (for example, medicine, social work, counseling) involves case conferences. Indeed, the amount of time spent in case conferences is best indicated in Murray Levine's advice that "all clinical installations need two staffs: one to go to meetings and the other to do the work." The case conference is the forum for sharing, discussing, and criticizing clinical tactics, conceptualizations, and goals. At their best, these case discussions forge and sustain collegiality and broaden horizons.

What startled me was that the tradition of the case conference did not exist in the schools. No teacher had a classroom lacking a child about whom he or she was puzzled; most of them had a disturbing number of such children, fewer than would be the case today. Even more startling was the stated reluctance of teachers to "refer" these children to anyone (for example, the principal, the pupil personnel department) for fear that it would be viewed as a sign of inadequacy. It was also true that many teachers did not make referrals either because "nothing will happen," or it would be weeks before someone "saw the child," or that when someone did see the child, no one would have a discussion with the teacher before or after. There was no forum where teachers and others with an obvious interest in or responsibility for the child could get together. Teachers were alone with their problems, theirs and their students. This was not only because of the pressures of time or lack of special services but also because the rationale for the case conference was not part of the school culture. By rationale I mean more than the potential benefits such a forum can provide for individual children. No less important is what it contributes to staff in regard to their learning, professional growth, collegiality, and sense of worthiness. It is a forum that says to staff: "You have knowledge, experience, or opinions that you are expected to articulate; you have a responsibility to yourself, your colleagues, your students, and your school." Case conferences are (usually) not decision-making affairs. They involve, among other things, ideas, actions, and values. At their best they are mind openers, forums one looks forward to— quite unlike faculty meetings described by one teacher as examples of man's inhumanity to man.

I am aware that time is a precious commodity in schools, and that schools do not have overflowing budgets. But I am also aware that considerations of time and money are clear indices of the scaling of aims, or values, or priorities. From their inception our public schools have never assigned importance to the intellectual, professional, and career needs of their personnel. However the aims of the schools were articulated, there was never any doubt that schools existed for children. If, as I have asserted, it is virtually impossible to create and sustain over time conditions for productive learning for students when they do not exist for teachers, the benefits sought by educational reform stand little chance of being realized.

The reader will encounter two obstacles to accepting what I have said. The first is simply in entertaining the possibility that schools should exist coequally for the development of students and educational personnel. It is a possibility that challenges long-standing beliefs held by these personnel and the public generally. One can point to examples in history (for example, women in relation to the world of work and ideas, the employment of children in the labor force, the absence of social security, national insurance for the elderly and others, the sixty- or seventy-hour work week, and so on) where challenges to what seemed right, natural, and proper were rejected out of hand. These and other examples are indirectly relevant but not particularly analogous because these challenges to customary thinking and practice rested primarily on moral grounds. These were challenges that had some grounding in our religious, legal, and constitutional history—that is, they essentially said that as a society we were not consistent with our fundamental beliefs, and that we were violating basic societal values of fairness, opportunity, and justice. Even so, it took decades of social turmoil and attitudinal change for these moral challenges to get reflected in our legal system. But morality is not the basis for my challenge to the unreflective belief that schools do and should exist primarily for children. Rather, the basis is that for our schools to do better than they do we have to give up the belief that it is possible to create the conditions for productive learning when those conditions do not exist for educational personnel.

Now to the second and, on the surface, more thorny obstacle. It is thorny because I have never had a serious, sustained discussion of this issue with anyone who, in the abstract, did not agree with my position. As one parent said to me: "That's a glimpse of the obvious, isn't it?" One can write human history as a saga of the inability to recognize the obvious. If my experience is any guide, the obvious is the bittersweet fruit of repetitive failures.

The second obstacle inheres in the recognition that the public generally and educators in particular are not "ready" to meet the challenge. It is easy to say that schools should exist coequally for students and educators. But what does that mean in practice? What are starting points? Neither question has clear answers. We are here not dealing with a problem that has a precise solution, as in arithmetic, a problem we do not have to solve again and again. In the realm of social affairs (societal, interpersonal, institutional), we are always dealing with problems we have to keep solving. Unlearning old attitudes, acquiring new ones, accepting new responsibilities, trying the new and risking failure, unrealistic time perspectives and expectations, limited resources, struggles as a consequence of altered power relationships—all this in a fishbowl into which are peering diverse groups whose understanding and support are as varied and complicating as they are necessary.

Of the two obstacles, the more difficult is the first one, because it requires us to change our view about whom schools are for. Such a change will not come about easily for several reasons (if it comes about at all). For one thing, such a change is so radical in its implications that most people will shrink from pursuing it. Second, there are no prescribed ways of overcoming this obstacle. Third, precisely because it is no less an obstacle for educators than for the general public, efforts to overcome it will be predictably conflictful, controversial, and both resisted and resented. Fourth, again precisely because it concerns our schools—in regard to which reform efforts have always been marked by the hard sell, unrealistic time perspectives, egregiously unsophisticated conceptions of the school culture, and confusion between appearance and reality—the efforts to overcome the first obstacle will be subject to similar mistakes. As I said earlier, educators and the public are not ready to confront, let alone think through, the thesis that schools must be coequally accommodating to the development of teachers and students. I am in no way suggesting, however, that we sit back and wait until that magical moment when public opinion polls tell us that people are "ready." That kind of argument is as ludicrous, insensitive, and ultimately self-defeating as when it was in earlier times presented to women, Blacks, and handicapped people.

There is one obvious and essential feature of readiness: the idea has to be in the marketplace, it has to have some currency, it has to have sellers seeking buyers. The obstacle I am discussing lacks these features. In light of that, it makes no sense to offer a prescription for what it would mean in practice for schools to exist coequally for students and teachers. I would have no difficulty coming up with such a prescription, but it would be the first and very brief chapter in a book detailing the operations of Murphy's and Sullivan's laws. (There are too many physicians who give prescriptions to patients without inquiring about their allergies, previous illnesses, and understanding of what is being given them, and, too frequently, without saying anything about possible side effects.) I trust that the reader will comprehend my reluctance to offer a prescription in regard to a problem that is not regarded as a problem! And that is the point of this chapter: the complete inability of educational reformers to examine the possibility that to create and sustain for children the conditions for productive growth without those conditions existing for educators is virtually impossible. If that is true, wholly or in large part, it is because we have so overlearned the standard answer to why and for whom schools exist that we have been rendered no less inadequate than our students in regard to critical thinking.

Contrary to what some readers might think, this chapter has not been an indulgence of fantasy. It is a direct outgrowth of coping with the intractability of schools to educational reform. As soon as one takes intractability seriously—if only as a possibility deserving scrutiny—one is not likely to come up with explanations in terms of faulty legislation, inadequate budgets, impoverished curricula, lowered standards of performance, poor quality of personnel, or a society seemingly intent on going to hell. Although these explanations are not wholly without merit, they explain little or nothing about intractability. Intractability is the hallmark of problems for which customary assumptions and axioms are no longer valid, if they ever were. Intractability says: "The problem is not technical. Nor is it motivational. Nor is it moral. The problem inheres in your unreflective acceptance of assumptions and axioms that seem so obviously right, natural, and proper that to question them is to question your reality. Therefore, faced with failure after failure, having tried this, that, and almost everything else, you don't examine your bedrock assumptions. Instead, you come up with variations on past themes—now with more desperation and anger, but less hope. Instead of stimulating discussion in which no assumption is sacred, no alternative automatically off limits, and arguments for practicality and the status quo are no inhibitors of envisioning alternatives, intractability has reinforced the repetition compulsion."

Let me illustrate the argument by analogy. Imagine that it is 1950 and you are at a national convention of the American Association on Mental Deficiency. In the midst of the proceedings someone gets up and says:

> I make a motion that this association go on record as being opposed to the institutionalization of mentally deficient individuals. These institutions are hellholes that are inimical to development and rehabilitation. They are warehouses for those our society rejects, does not comprehend, and isolates in institutions deliberately built in the middle of nowhere. There is no evidence whatsoever that they accomplish any purpose other than isolating these individuals. In the middle of the nineteenth century, Dorothea Dix described to the Massachusetts legislature the inhumane conditions in our so-called humane institutions. These conditions continue today. When these conditions are exposed, there are frantic, well-intentioned efforts to improve these institutions. The clamor for reform subsides only to rise again when it is apparent that conditions changed but did not improve. It has been noted at this meeting, with a good deal of alarm, that there ap-

pears to be a tendency for parents to use our courts in an effort to change and improve conditions. But no one is saying that we should rethink whether we need these institutions, whether it is possible truly to bring about and sustain desired change, whether it is both possible and necessary to maintain these individuals in their communities. Because we have these institutions is no excuse to use them as we have, to continue to fly in the face of their intractability to improvement.

The response to this impassioned speech would have been fourfold. First, the hat would have been passed for contributions to subsidize psychotherapy or institutionalization for the speechmaker. Second, there would be acknowledgment that these institutions were far from sources of satisfaction but that the task was to repair, not eliminate, them. Third, if they were in need of repair, it reflected the niggardliness of legislatures and the public generally—that is, an unwillingness to appropriate funds to do the job well. Fourth, granted that many residents did not need to be in institutions, the glaring fact was that society was not ready to accommodate to their needs in their communities.

Beginning in the fifties, and with increasing frequency, these kinds of institutions came under the jurisdiction of our courts. In 1969 Burton Blatt was invited by the governor to address the Massachusetts legislature on what these institutions were like, based on his studies of them in three states. He essentially repeated Dorothea Dix's address but with photographs. Ten years later he revisited these same institutions. The photographs indicate that conditions were "cleaner" but little else had changed despite efforts at repair (Blatt, 1970a, 1970b).

It was correct to say that society was not ready for the deinstitutionalization of mentally retarded individuals. It was no less correct to say that there were citizens in that same society who came to see that these institutions were intractable to improvement. And it was these citizens, organized into groups, who in large measure (there were other factors) contributed to the speed of deinstitutionalization. But what should not be glossed over is the fact that the officials pressured into carrying out deinstitutionalization were not ready either in terms of knowledge of communities, or values, or realistic programming. Those charged with overseeing the process knew institutions; they did not know communities. In truth, no one was really "ready." Deinstitutionalization gathered momentum not because anyone was clear about the universe of alternatives that could or should be considered, but because it was powered by legal, economic, and moral pressures confronting the fact of intractability. So if deinstitutionalization of the mentally retarded has been far from a success, it does speak to the issues of readiness. If that is the case, the fact remains that no knowledgeable person will assert that we should return to creating or rebuilding the institutions of the past. My imaginary 1950 speechmaker did not need psychotherapy or shock treatment because he challenged axioms undergirding the thinking of the times. He was correct that the historical evidence supported a conclusion of intractability. He should be pardoned for not envisioning how lack of readiness on the part of everyone would inevitably produce very mixed results. But lack of readiness is no excuse for inaction or silence. To wait for readiness is to wait for Godot. Understandably, we like to believe that our efforts at significant reform will accomplish our goals—soon, smoothly, unproblematically, no three steps forward and two steps backward. If such hopes are understandable, they also betray a lack of understanding of what significant institutional and societal change entails.

In regard to my argument that schools are no less for the growth of staff than for students, I am in the same position as that of my 1950 speechmaker. There is one difference, however. Whenever and wherever I have presented my argument, I have gotten the sense that many people intuitively agreed with me. It is by no means alien to my experience over the decades to have people tell me that I was wrong, egregiously or otherwise. But in the past two decades when this argument was percolating in my head and I took advantage of countless opportunities to articulate it to others, no one has ever disagreed with what I said. It has the ring of truth, a face validity.

But if no one has disagreed, it is also the case that no one considered the argument "realistic" or "practical," but rather one, like so many others, that requires a utopia for its spirit to be reflected appropriately in action. And so we are back to the lack of readiness! No one is ready.

We are beginning to hear much these days about the benefits to be derived from giving teachers a greatly enlarged role in changing and running schools. (If we are beginning to hear much, it says more about the ability of a few individuals to use or have access to mass media than it does about acceptance, which is minimal. Nor should one underestimate the potential significance of the Illinois legislation that essentially lessens the decision-making power of all school personnel.) As indicated in an earlier chapter, these few sites are not being studied in a way (if they are being studied at all) that will permit us to draw conclusions about what has happened or is happening. Please note that I said study and not evaluate. To evaluate requires that we have as comprehensive a picture as is practically possible about the developmental processes of creation and implementation. *That* we do not and are not likely to have. But on the basis of some limited observations, less limited conversation with participants, and anecdotal reports in the mass media, one conclusion seems to emerge: there is agreement that the sole outcome by which these alterations in power are being and will be judged is what happens to the achievement test scores of students. That these alterations in power may have beneficial effects for the sense of worthiness and growth of staff is a desirable outcome only if it contributes to the elevation of test scores. That this elevation has not taken place (there are, apparently, the usual few exceptions) has had the predictable effect of a somewhat frantic, increased focusing on student performance. I am reminded here of my colleague Edward Zigler who helped initiate Headstart, was the first director of the federal Office of Child Development, and more than any other person, has helped protect that program from vicissitudes in the political arena. He relates that when he would go before a congressional committee in support of the program, which included meals for Headstart children, it was not sufficient to justify funds for meals on the basis that many children came to the program ill-fed and hungry. He had to justify it on the basis that the meals would contribute to improved learning. He, of course, knew better than that. Just as a full stomach stands in no direct relationship to productive learning, alterations in power relationships in no way ensure that the contextual ingredients that together stimulate and sustain student interest, curiosity, and perseverance will be altered. Alterations in power relationships—be they in favor of increased parental influence, or teachers, or of a new conglomeration of groups—are just that: alterations in power. Why these alterations? For whom are these alterations relevant? What is there about these alterations to suggest that they are intended to change the traditional classroom in ways no less significant for students than for staff? Should we not recognize and be concerned about the obvious fact that alterations in power are alterations among groups who differ very little in their thinking in regard to whom schools are for and how they should be judged? Alterations in power that are not explicitly intended to alter, among other things, the structure and atmosphere of the traditional classroom, will have little or no effect on student performance (which I do not equate with test scores). As I shall indicate in the next chapter, reform efforts have been stimulated by concern about inadequate test scores. They have not been stimulated by concern for lack of student interest and curiosity, except as such lacks are interpreted as reflecting low teacher expectations, a nondemanding curriculum, poorly educated teachers, the inadequate technical skills of teachers, family instability, and what I can only describe as the opposite of a shape-up-or-ship-out attitude of school personnel. *Whatever factors, variables, and ambience are conducive for the growth, development, and self-regard of a school's staff are precisely those that are crucial to obtaining the same consequences for students in a classroom.* To focus on the latter and ignore or gloss over the former is an invitation to disillusionment.

## Notes

1. This and other themes in this chapter were taken up at length in *The Creation of Settings and the Future Societies,* published in 1972 by Jossey-Bass and reprinted in paperback in 1988 by Brookline Books, Cambridge, Mass.
2. Transcripts of some of these meetings can be found in S. B. Sarason and others, *Psychology in Community Settings* (New York: Wiley, 1966).
3. Without question, Farber's forthcoming (1991) book on teacher burnout is the most comprehensive, analytic, and instructive book on the topic, and I urge the reader to study it. He places the problem in the context of the culture of the school, enabling the reader to avoid the too frequent mistake of viewing burnout phenomena only in terms of an asocial individual psychology. And he does not refrain, if only because the literature is so compelling, from concluding that current efforts at educational reform are very likely to be disappointing. Indeed, his book contains a wealth of evidence for what I have said in these pages. His is truly a creative scholarly effort that, I predict, will stand the test of time. I wish to thank Professor Farber for allowing me to see his manuscript before it was published.

# 9

# AN OVERARCHING GOAL
# FOR STUDENTS

THERE IS, IN MY OPINION, AN OVERARCHING GOAL WE SHOULD
have for students. Although I am not downplaying the importance of other major goals; I consider the overarching goal to
be one that, if not achieved and sustained, impoverishes educational experience not only during the school years but also
in the years thereafter. Let me use as a text for this final ser-
mon the "mission statement" issued by the New Rochelle (New
York) public schools in June 1987.

> The mission of the New Rochelle School System, acknowl-
> edging its richly complex history, is to produce responsi-
> ble, self-sufficient citizens who possess the self-esteem, ini-
> tiative, skills, and wisdom to continue individual growth,
> pursue knowledge, develop aesthetic sensibilities, and value
> cultural diversity by providing intellectually challenging
> educational programs that celebrate change but affirm
> tradition and promote excellence through an active part-
> nership with the community, a comprehensive and re-
> sponsive curriculum, and a dedicated and knowledge-
> able staff.

**155**

That is an exemplary mission statement in three respects. First, it identifies the major stakeholders in the educational enterprise, suggesting that the mission is incapable of realization if any of them is absent or relegated to a secondary role. The phrases "an active partnership with the community" and "celebrate change but affirm tradition" have the virtue of suggesting that the boundaries between the community, on the one hand, and the encapsulated school and its encapsulated classrooms, on the other hand, will become far more porous than heretofore. In the context of the mission statement, these phrases are not intended, I assume, to imply that the role of the community is only to support educators to do what they want to do. Comprised as it is of individuals and groups, containing as it does resources and sites relevant to educational goals, the community can be used to change and enhance the experience of students. Mission statements are not prescriptions for action and, therefore, we cannot say what "active partnership with the community" means in this instance. It is fashionable today to be in favor of such an active partnership, although far more often than not such assent on the part of educators means: "How can we get them to support what we are already doing?" At least in the case of the New Rochelle statement, the partnership is for the purpose of change. So, if one were to study New Rochelle schools before the mission statement was publicized and for subsequent years, one should be able to discern changes in relationships among the stakeholders—that is, the quality, substance, and frequency of relationships and the ways in which the different resources of the stakeholders are exploited. Exploited for what purpose? That brings us to the second and more fundamental respect in which the mission statement is refreshing, if not novel. Indeed, of the hundreds of such statements I have read (fortunately, most mission statements are brief), I cannot recall one that says so clearly that the overarching goal is to engender and sustain in students a desire "to continue individual growth, pursue knowledge, develop aesthetic sensibilities . . . by providing intellectually challenging programs." It is noteworthy that such goals are hardly captured or measured by our usual tests.

However atypically refreshing the New Rochelle mission statement is, I have to fault it on two grounds. The first is that, consistent with what I said in the previous chapter, the statement reinforces the axiom that schools exist primarily (really exclusively) for students. No more on that matter! The second is that it begs the question: why have schools not "produced" the citizens envisioned in the statement? I do not expect a mission statement to answer that question, and one should be satisfied that the statement suggests that change is in order—that is, what is should no longer be, and what the statement envisions will not be realized under existing structures and practices. But I have to raise that question in order to point out that many of the characteristics of students that the mission statement seeks to engender are already possessed by the students when they start school. Why do they get extinguished or go underground or get manifested outside of school?

If there is anything we can say about the biologically intact, preschool child, it is that he or she is a question-asking, question-answering, questing, knowledge-pursuing organism, pursuing knowledge about self, others, and its world. That is truly a glimpse of the obvious but, remarkably, it is not taken seriously. Our schools (beginning in kindergarten), in a myriad of ways and with the best of intentions, require the student to make a sharp distinction between "what I am interested in and what I am supposed to be interested in, what I am curious about and what I am supposed to be curious about, what I know and what I am supposed to know, what kinds of questions I would like to ask and what questions I am told I should or it is permissible to ask." Put more succinctly, schools do a remarkably effective job, albeit unwittingly, of getting children to conclude that there are two worlds—the one inside of school and the one outside—and they have no doubt whatsoever about which of the two is intrinsically more interesting and stimulating. It is probably the case that students have always drawn that conclusion, and it is not relevant here to try to decide to what extent the conclusion about two worlds is inevitable. But it is also the case that in this century, especially since World War II, the perceived gulf between the two worlds has widened and their contradictory or conflicting purposes (as perceived by students) have become more stark.

Let me now state what should be our overarching goal for students. I say "our" goal, but it is also one that students hold and which, they will tell you, is so poorly and infrequently approximated as to make classrooms very uninteresting places, intellectually and interpersonally. The overarching goal rests on the recognition that children start school with the expectation that their curiosity about a myriad of things—about people, places, growing up—will receive some answers. If you ask children why they are in school, they will not regurgitate a mission statement. They are likely to say that they are in school "to learn," for example, reading, writing, and arithmetic. Some come with feelings of awe, wonder, and excitement, others with an anxious enthusiasm, and some with a fearful reluctance. For all of them, however, school is a source of curiosity and expectations. We can legitimately describe starting school as a rite of passage, the crossing of a dividing line separating a known from an unknown world, moving from a familiar role of existence to an unfamiliar but desirable role with new tasks and responsibilities. Albeit inchoately, children know that life will now be different for them in terms of their responsibilities and the expectations of others. If they know, as they do, that they will be learning, they expect that it will be challenging, interesting, and meaningful. And to the young child, learning means what it means for any learner regardless of age: it will in diverse ways make personal sense in relation to one's interests, questions, skills, and growth. And to "make sense" means concrete sense, that sense of possession and of illumination that carries one willingly forward. It is, apparently, easy to overlook the fact that children have two truly burning interests: themselves and the social world around them. And in regard to each, their questions are both concrete and countless.

All of the above is, once again, obvious, but if one were to observe classrooms from kindergarten onward, one would be hard put to find instances where the obvious is being taken seriously. I have illustrated this in earlier chapters. Two more examples will suffice here.

President Kennedy was assassinated on a Friday. In New Haven, schools remained closed until the following Wednesday. That was the day of the week I met with a group of new teachers (as described in the previous chapter) after the school day. When I entered the clinic conference room, the teachers were talking to each other, rather excitedly, about what they had experienced that day in their classrooms. And what were they talking about? They were voicing their reactions to the assassination and saying that, from the standpoint of learning, it had been a fruitless day because children seemed unable to attend to their tasks. No teacher denied that the assassination took center stage in the minds of the children. No teacher really expected that when the children came to school that day they would be other than overflowing with questions about the assassination. And yet, the teachers proceeded "to try to teach" as if it were a normal day. There was a curriculum, there was a lesson plan, and they took precedence, as if what was gripping the students was irrelevant to educational purposes.

Fortunately, assassinations are infrequent events. If the example is an extreme one, it is nevertheless not atypical of how what is interesting to children so infrequently gets reflected and exploited in learning. How many times in this century has it been said that "you teach children, not subject matter"? When that is said, it is intended to emphasize that learning is arid, unproductive, and stifling to the degree that it does not take into account the interests, curiosity, and questions of the learner. To the degree that classroom learning requires of children that they conform to what others say is important, learn it in ways that others say is the way to learn, and separate this learning from all other contexts of experience and learning children bring to school, the school then is remarkably and predictably effective in getting children to regard the classroom as an uninteresting place. That does not mean that children do not learn what others say they should learn, although it is obvious that a fair number do not. It means that what they learn (what tests measure) is not viewed by students with a sense of growth or achievement but as the overcoming of hurdles in a compulsory obstacle course, which when traversed presumably frees one to pursue one's real interests. In the words of the New Rochelle mission statement, it does not produce citizens who desire "to continue individual growth," certainly not in the educational arena.

A second example is more personal. On the second or third day of my geometry class in high school, the teacher drew two connecting lines on the blackboard and said: "That is an obtuse angle." Why is it called *obtuse?* Why that word and not some other word? Why a word that I had never heard before? Why should I care about obtuse angles or, for that matter, geometry? What does geometry *mean?* Who invented the curse of geometry and what relation did it have to anything in my world? That geometry course stimulated more unanswered questions in me than any other course before or since. In that sense, it was a stimulating course! But it was also a course in which I was in an ever-enveloping fog, and I almost flunked it. One secure conclusion resulted: only under the threat of death would I take another math class. And I did not, until my last year of college when I needed a four-point course and the only one that I could fit into my schedule was Richard Henry's math course. I had come to know Professor Henry, a most delightful, funny, challenging, and creative individual. When will you take a course with me, he would ask? I told him about geometry but promised that when hell froze over, I would take his course. If I wanted to graduate, I needed his four-point course. It was quite an experience. For one thing, he was amazingly sensitive to what today we call "math anxiety." Second, any question was on limits, not off, however foolish you might think it was. Third, if you were having difficulty, it was your obligation to say it out loud and his responsibility to help you. Fourth, I never got the feeling that his pace was determined by a curriculum, only by where you and others were. His job, and he said so explicitly and his actions were consistent with what he said, was not only to help you learn math but also to understand and enjoy it. Fifth, and in some ways the most psychologically significant point, he never began with abstractions or formulas that we had to memorize but rather with concrete examples (or tasks) with which we could easily identify from personal experience. He had the most masterful grasp of the need for and the processes required for going from the concrete to the abstract, and he knew how to stimulate students to use their concrete experience.

I know that there are few Richard Henrys among math teachers, but that is not the point of the example. The point is that he taught students, not subject matter, and that is a feature lacking almost totally in teachers generally, including those in higher education. I have observed mathematics and science courses in many public schools, and my dominant reaction is that these courses are reflections of curricula aimed at the achievement of an efficient rote memory at the expense of interest and meaning. Countless other observers would agree. I am not scapegoating teachers or any other group. Teachers teach the way they have been taught, and those who teach them teach the way they have been taught, and so on. Children who begin school are nascent scientists and artists. They are already formed and forming explorers of themselves and their world. That is far more overtly clear in relation to artistic than to scientific activity, but those are surface differences. The preschool years are the awe and wonder years: Why do clouds move? Why is the sky blue? What keeps an airplane in the sky? How do they make pictures on a TV screen? How can you talk to someone who is far away? How are babies made? How are they born? Why do boys have a penis and girls do not? What is a germ? How to you "catch" a cold? Why do people fight? Where is God? If you say there is no God, then who made the world? What is a dream? Why are they sometimes so scary?

My most recent book, *The Challenge of Art to Psychology* (1990), deals with the question: if developmental research is correct that artistic activity is universal among young children—and the evidence for that conclusion is overwhelming—why does interest in that activity decline drastically when schooling begins? The relevance of that book to the present one is indicated by the fact that one of the chapter headings in that earlier book is "The Predictable Failure of Education Reform." But that chapter has to do with efforts to reform art education. In the present book the argument is made more generally. That young children are question-asking, answer-seeking characters is among the most obvious features of human development. And that is true regardless of family, race, ethnicity, economic background, or where on this earth children are found. When children start school, a message is conveyed to them that is as influential as it is subtle and unverbalized: "Forget or set aside your world of questions and interests. Your job, our responsibility, is to get you to learn rules, facts, and skills, without which you are nothing. School is not for play or for dreaming. It is work, serious work. And if you pay attention, work hard, some day when you are big, you will understand." There is a distinction between work and labor. To labor, as on an assembly line, is to engage in an activity the products of which in no way reflect characteristics of the laborer; the relation between laborer and product is completely impersonal. To work is to engage in an activity that, in some way to some degree, bears the imprimatur of the worker. To most children, not all, school is where you labor, where much of your world of interests and curiosity becomes alien or unrelated to what you are required to do. School does not extinguish in children the interests and probings of that "other world." That is impossible. What school does is erect a barrier between two worlds, a kind of Berlin Wall that seems in no danger of being torn down.

The overarching aim of schooling should be to recognize, capitalize on, and exploit the obvious fact that children come to school already possessed of the major psychological attributes crucial to productive learning. They are thinkers and doers before they come to school. They are eager to remain thinkers and doers, to integrate new worlds into their old ones—an integration not a separation. They already know that there is much they do not know and are eager to learn. Motivation is not a problem. They want to conform, but to them conformity does not mean giving up or setting aside the world most familiar and intriguing to them. There is a difference between willing conformity and an unwilling and puzzled submission. That children generally experience school as boring and uninteresting should occasion no surprise. What would require explanation is if they felt otherwise.

What is at stake here is what happens to children not only during the school years in regard to this overarching aim but in their adult years as well. The aim of education is not simply to keep students in school and to graduate them, just as the aim of imprisonment of criminals is not to make sure that they serve their sentences. On the level of rhetoric, we are told that the aim of imprisonment is to reduce the likelihood that the criminal will engage in illegal activities once the sentence is served. The realities, unfortunately, contradict the rhetoric. Analogously, we want students to do more and learn more than is symbolized by a diploma or test scores. Surely no one would disagree with this excerpt from the New Rochelle mission statement: "to produce responsible, self-sufficient citizens who possess the self-esteem, initiative, skills, and *wisdom to continue individual growth [and] pursue knowledge.*" Should not our aim be to judge whatever we do for children in our schools by the criterion of how we are fostering the desire to continue to learn about self, others, and the world, to live in the world of ideas and possibilities, to see the life span as an endless intellectual and personal quest for knowledge and meaning? Should we not be upset that so many students come to view the life of the mind, the world of ideas, the history of man, as derogated arenas of experience?

The educational reform movement, today and in the past, has not come to grips with this overarching aim. One can alter curricula, change power relationships, raise standards, and do a lot more, but if these efforts are not powered by altered conceptions of what children are and what makes them tick and keeps them intellectually alive, willingly pursuing knowledge and growth, their results will be inconsequential. As I said earlier, the problem is a long-standing one, but precisely because the worlds in and out of school have become increasingly separated, and the school world suffers by comparison in terms of interest, stimulation, and motivation, the consequences of that separation are more dangerous for our society. Until the sixties it was valid to say that education reform was cyclical—that is, about every decade or so the fire for reform (which never went out) would become a four-alarm blaze that the society sought to extinguish. Since the sixties, however, the reform movement has never been far from societal center stage. What has happened is that every segment of our society has come to see, although for diverse reasons, that the inadequacies of our schools are having and will continue to have untoward consequences for the health of the social fabric and the changing relationship of the society to the rest of the world. The concern is warranted, but when I read the plethora of reports that essentially recommend what has been recommended and done before (variations on a few themes notwithstanding), I see no indication that the overarching aim I stated, and which has been stated by many others in the past, is acknowledged and taken seriously. And by this I mean two things. First, you must understand and digest the fact that children, all children come to school motivated to enlarge their worlds. You start with *their* worlds.[1] You do not look at them, certainly not initially, as organisms to be molded and regulated. You look at them to determine how what they are, seek to know, and have experienced can be used as the fuel to fire the process for enlargement of interests, knowledge, and skills. You do not look at them from the perspective of a curriculum, classroom, or school structure. You enter their world to comprehend and reinforce the psychological assets they already possess. You do not look at them in terms of deficits: what they do not know but need to know. Far from having deficits, they are asset rich. You enter their world in order to aid them and you to build bridges between two worlds, not walls. Second, if you take the first point seriously, you are required not to start with an unreflective acceptance of schools as we know them but rather with the question: what should schools be in order to accomplish what pursuit of the first point suggests? As long as you start the reform effort with that unreflective acceptance of the culture, traditions, and organization of classrooms and schools as we know them, the implications of the first point will not surface. If you take that first point seriously, you will find yourself asking: if we were to start from scratch, what would schools look like? But, it can be argued, we are not starting from scratch. We have schools. How do we begin to change schools to make them more consistent with that first point? That question sounds more practical, not an exercise in wishful thinking. In my experience, those who ask that presumably more practical question— usually saying that to disagree with my overarching aim is to be for sin and against virtue—have no comprehension of the radical changes that would be required in all of those variables that are part of the educational enterprise. When I point out what some of those changes might be and the time perspective one must adopt in regard to them—the obstacles that will be encountered, the resistances, the experience we need to gain to learn from failure, the knowledge that where we want to go in no clear way tells us how to get there—they react to me as if all of my genes convérged to produce a wet blanket. What they seek are answers, and by answers they mean elevations in test scores. Although they regard the overarching aim as obviously virtuous, they are both unable and unwilling to confront two questions: What is there about classrooms and schools that is inimical to that aim? Why should we expect that the reforms now being proposed will positively support that aim? Today the fashionable buzzword is "restructuring." Granted that restructuring (whatever that may mean) is necessary, and granted that it can have desirable consequences for parents and educators, on what basis, other than hope and prayer, will it bring about classrooms consistent with the overarching aim?

Here is a concrete example of my argument. In the *Michigan Law Review* of 1989 (Vol. 87) there is an article by Joseph Singer of the faculty of the Boston University School of Law. The title of the article is "Persuasion." In truth, it is an article about the kind of productive learning that is consistent with, a derivative of, the overarching aim. Although what he describes takes place in a classroom in a law school, it is in every respect relevant to any classroom anywhere.

Here is a situation that Singer presents to his class:

A factory has operated in a city for more than fifty years. The city has grown up around the factory and has come to rely upon it, as have its employees. The company has benefited enormously from its long-term relationship with the workers and the community. Yet the company appears unconcerned for their welfare. Instead, its officers focus on the bottom line; their only goal is to maximize profits and returns to shareholders. Ruled by a distant and seemingly unapproachable board of directors, the company closes the factory, putting thousands of people out of work, many of them permanently. The city faces a crisis. Many people experience downward mobility. Even most of those who find work face reduced living standards. All of the workers face grave difficulties in putting their lives back together.

It is a story of betrayal. The workers trusted the company and depended on it. The company lived off that trust, took advantage of it, and finally, abused it.

Most of the students did not agree with the conclusion of betrayal. No one was unsympathetic to the plight of the workers and the community, but almost all of the students justified the closing on three grounds: managerial prerogatives, freedom of contract, and deference to the legislature. "Conservative students are relatively confident and open about their beliefs in limited government." Liberal students "worry about how we, as a society, treat vulnerable people in times of crisis; yet they are embarrassed, almost apologetic, about their advocacy of government regulation." In effect, the students reacted to the case in terms of narrow, abstract legal principles, although it was emotionally troubling. Legal principles, they learn in law schools, are and should be independent of, not distorted by, personal values, experience, and emotions. As Justice Holmes reminded a young lawyer appearing before the Supreme Court for the first time, and who made much, in his argument, of serving justice, "Young man, we are here to serve the law, not justice."

Singer was puzzled by the difficulty he had in getting the students to understand that the argument for government regulation of plant closings was legally and personally thorny and complex. What, he asked himself, was missing from his failed educational aim? His answer was: "The students understood intellectually that unregulated plant closings cause significant problems and create many victims. But they understood those victims through distanced analytic language; they were "externalities" rather than people with whom they could empathize." So when he taught the course the following year, he gave the students the same set of readings but this time he did not mention the problem of plant closings. Instead, he said:

This did not happen, but suppose it did happen. For some time now, the faculty of the law school has been worried about the declining competence of attorneys. Chief Justice Warren Burger has voiced concerns about the preparation and competence of the Supreme Court bar. Recent scandals have arisen involving lawyer neglect of client matters, violation of ethical norms, and even violations of law. We have therefore commissioned a study to investigate how legal education can contribute to protecting the public from unprepared or unethical lawyers. Our study indicates that the bottom third of our graduating class will never be truly competent at the complexities of the practice of law. This situation demands a remedy. Your examinations for the first year of law school are next week. As a consumer protection measure, we intend to give failing grades to the bottom thirty-three percent of the class. The bottom third will flunk out of school. The old way of doing things was right. Look to the left of you; look to the right of you. One of you will not be here in the fall. You are free to apply to transfer to other law schools, but we will not recommend you to them. In fact, if they ask us, we will candidly inform them that we are pessimistic about your ability to make it in the profession. We recognize that this new policy is a substantial change from our previous grading curve, under which only two to three percent of each class would be asked not to return. We know that many of you will be surprised and disappointed at our change in policy. Nonetheless, it is a necessary measure to promote the efficient delivery of legal services.

You bring a lawsuit, asking the court to order the law school to allow you to graduate on the basis of the rules that were in effect at the time you accepted our offer to come here. Do you have any rights?

Students reacted "with alarm." "They overwhelmingly feel that a sudden change of policy like this is fundamentally unfair, and that they should be entitled to relief. The feeling is not always unanimous, although sometimes it is. . . . It is clear that those who take a hard-line, antiregulatory approach here understand that the burden of proof is on them."

Let us not be detained by the pro and con legal arguments that Singer and the students discuss, except to say that his pedagogical goal is not to indoctrinate. I chose the example because it describes why and how a particular teacher sought to make a connection between learning and thinking about abstract principles and the lives of the students. And it is clear that, far from sacrificing quantity and quality of subject matter, the subject matter became a spur to further learning. Singer was teaching not subject matter but students who had experiential assets that could make the subject provocatively meaningful—that is, consistent with the overarching aim.

In what ways is Singer an atypical teacher? For one thing, he had the courage to admit to himself that he was not reaching his students in ways he wanted for their growth. That really is not atypical because most classroom teachers are quite aware that they are falling short of their mark. In my experience, too many people have concluded that too many teachers are not as concerned as they should be about the performance of students. That is an unjustified and demeaning caricature. If many teachers burn out, it is a consequence of frustration and disappointment with the fruits of their efforts. Where Singer is atypical is in gaining the insight that the logic or structure of subject matter should, whenever possible, be related to something in the experience of students. There are classroom teachers who understand and act appropriately in regard to that insight. They are few in number, and for two major reasons. The first is the pressure teachers feel they are under to cover a curriculum, causing them to focus on subject matter and not students. That, of course, does not explain why some teachers are able to overcome or not succumb completely to such pressure. The second reason is that the formal preparation of teachers is grossly inadequate in helping them to understand and implement the insight. It is easy to state and agree with the overarching aim; it is not easy to comprehend it in that visceral way that gives stimulus and direction to action. Teachers are taught the way they have been taught in their preprofessional years and before.

No one who seeks to become a teacher is incapable of gaining the insight. That teachers, like any other professional group, will vary in the ease with which they gain the insight and in the quality of their efforts at implementation is not the issue. The issue is that the overarching aim and the insight it requires are far from central in their professional training. Earlier in this book I briefly discussed the intractability of medical schools to efforts at making issues surrounding caring and compassion more central to medical training. As a result, physicians who are caring and compassionate are that way despite their training, not because of it, which is why there are relatively few of them. I should point out that medical students are selected by criteria that absolutely have no relationship to the attributes of caring and compassion. We are far better off in regard to those who seek a career in education. In my experience, they seek such a career because they see the role of the teacher as quintessentially expressive of the desire to be caring and compassionate. But these are not superficial characteristics. What they require is the effort to comprehend someone else's world and to use that comprehension to help that individual. In the case of the teacher, that should mean comprehending and utilizing that which in a student's experience is relevant to the task at hand. I am obviously not suggesting that teachers become psychotherapists or philosophers, but that they be helped to understand their primary task (not their exclusive one) is to figure out how the experiences of students can be brought to bear on subject matter—that is, how to make the wall between two worlds more porous and permeable. That is no easy intellectual and personal task. Given the way our classrooms and schools are organized, the effect that has on teachers and students, and the values and goals that are dominant, the task is an impossible one.

On the very day (January 10, 1990) I write these words, the mass media are reporting the results of the most recent national assessment of student performance. The Secretary of Education deemed them "appalling." Scores had not declined, and he and others made valiant efforts to take heart that the test scores of this racial group or that age cohort had increased somewhat. (This is akin to the difference between being run down by a car going forty or one going forty-four miles an hour.) So what is to be done? The secretary proclaims that schools have to be restructured, that more groups have to be related to matters educational, and that we must do better than we are doing. His heart, not his head, is in the right place.

What if the results of the national assessment had been dramatically better? What would the secretary (and many others) have said? Does anyone doubt that he would have joyously said that we are on the road to recovery and that our major educational aims are being realized? It is important here that I emphasize that such a dramatic improvement would be cause for satisfaction. Having said that, I must go on to say that such improvement in no way can be interpreted to mean that students are now more motivated to continue their intellectual growth, that they are more interested in the world of ideas and history, that they regard schooling more positively and enthusiastically, that they understand themselves and their worlds more deeply, that they are better "thinking" organisms, and that they have acquired those attributes that will make them better citizens and those attitudes and interests that will permit them productively to exploit themselves in a troublesome world. In brief, what do these improvements in test scores signify for the overarching aim I have stressed? The answer has to be in two parts. The first and most justified answer is that we do not know, and not knowing that (because we do not seek to know) speaks volumes about how seriously we take the overarching aim.

The second answer is that we have learned enough to know that changes in test scores can be due to factors, at least in part, that are not all that praiseworthy—for example, teaching for the test and emphasizing facts. So, for example, on the front page of the *New Haven Register* for January 6, 1990, there is the headline "Slight Gain Posted by Pupils on State Tests." In Connecticut these "mastery" tests for reading, writing, math, and language arts are administered to fourth, sixth, and eighth graders. The Commissioner of Education is quoted as saying: "I think we are upbeat and moving in the right direction. But we can't declare victory. We still have a long way to go." The article goes on to report that the commissioner "believes teachers have learned 'to teach for the test'—a practice educators usually criticize . . . because students may learn only what is necessary to pass, not a broad range of knowledge. But because the mastery tests evaluate dozens of specific skills, teaching for the tests means pupils are learning what they should know, the commissioner said." Knowledge and skills—attaining them is the aim of education! All else is a dispensable luxury, and that includes the overarching aim I have been discussing. Pour in the facts, hone their skills, measure them objectively, tote that bale, and old man river keeps on rolling along. With friends like that, education need never worry about enemies. And let us not scapegoat tests and testmakers whose business it is, after all, to give the policymakers what they want. It is not their business to change the priorities of their customers.

I have presented what I believe should be our overarching aim for students. It is not the sole aim of education, but it should require us to ensure that it informs and directs any other aim. Take, for example, the teaching of a foreign language, which some states (for example, New York) have mandated. I have sat in classrooms in which a foreign language was being taught. Predictably, the teaching rationale was no different from that for the more traditional subject matter in terms of how the classroom is organized, the length of a period, and the intervals between classes. Also predictably, because my observations were made in classes that were elective not compulsory, the students began with a good deal of interest and en-

thusiasm. (I could tell this story with my own experience in
Spanish and German classes when I was in high school, but I
will refrain except to say that it led me decades later to observe
these kinds of classrooms.) Interest and enthusiasm did not last
long, which is not to say that they were extinguished. But in
the main these became joyless affairs as the students became
mired in matters of grammar and conjugation, as the gulf between what they were learning and what they wanted to learn
widened. Learning a foreign language—its structural logic, id-
ioms, inflections, and those inevitable exceptions to the usual
rules—is no easy matter. There is no way you can learn without struggle. In any event, neither the teachers nor the students I observed were satisfied with what was going on. The
students were dutiful and respectful, but not very motivated.
To say that they had been "engaged" would truly be an over-
statement. The teachers were painfully aware of this, but a curriculum is a curriculum and they rarely diverged from it.

With one of these teachers I felt I could be intrusively direct, and so I said to her: "Neither you nor your students seem
all that happy about the class. Is there not another way to think
about it? Forget you are in a school. What if it were summer
and the parents of these children asked you to teach them
Spanish and you had them all day for a month or so and you
could teach them in any way you wanted. Would it look like an
intensive version of this classroom?" To which she replied
(paraphrased): "You are right. I am not happy with the class.
But then again, I never am satisfied. These are a good bunch
of kids. The problem is that I have them for forty-minute periods three times a week. Except for these periods, they live in
a world of English. What would I do if I had them all day,
everyday, in the summer? The short answer is that we would,
for a good part of that time, *live* Spanish. No grammar or anything like that. That's the way I learned Spanish, and quickly,
when in my junior year in college I lived for a year with a
family in Mexico. I knew next to nothing about Spanish, and
their English was no better. It was quite an experience that for
the first week or so was both frustrating and exciting. After
the first week, I was sorry I came. After a month, I was amazed
that I had become semi-fluent. I had my Spanish books and

dictionary, which during that first month were not all that helpful. So what would I do in the summer with kids like these? We would live Spanish and we would have a ball. They would eat it up. I can just see the looks on their faces as they hear themselves conversing in real Spanish."

I then asked her, with as deadpan an expression as I could muster, "Why can't that be done during the school year?" In staring disbelief, she answered: "Are you kidding? How could that be possible the way school days are organized? They have to take other courses. How could they be freed for a month to learn only Spanish? It simply is not possible." She was right, of course. Once one accepts the traditional way in which high schools are organized—which means accepting a number of dubious assumptions about factors that make for productive learning—then my question is nonsensical. But if it is nonsensical, her answer explicitly concedes that by virtue of the way the school is organized, she and her students are short-changed. Both have to conform to that organization. The organization cannot conform to what this teacher considers a more productive way of learning Spanish, a quicker way, not a way of convincing students that learning a foreign language is not for them. So the question becomes: Are there ways of thinking about the organization of schools that would make it more possible to try and evaluate contexts for learning that hold promise of being more consistent with the overarching aim? If you start by accepting the present structure, if you insist that those who seek to change it must guarantee ahead of time that it will work, you guarantee one thing: nothing will change. If you unreflectively assume that the psychological rationale undergirding the present structure is valid in whole or in part, you possess all of the attributes necessary to reinforce the status quo.

The man from Mars may be helpful here. He was inordinately helpful to me, which is why he occupies an important role in my book, *The Culture of the School and the Problem of Change*.

Imagine that the man from Mars is in a space platform hovering over a school. He does not know English, cannot hear anything, but he can see everything and everyone in that school. He is curious about everything he sees in the school which, needless to say, he does not comprehend. But he has the most avant garde computers which he puts to work in an effort to make sense of what is going on. He feeds the computer myriads of data organized into myriads of categories which are then statistically intercorrelated in wall-to-wall fashion, permitting him to discern regularities—that is, to discern features that predictably recur. What regularities would he become aware of?

The most obvious is the five-two regularity: for five consecutive days the school is one of the most densely populated settings; for two consecutive days it is devoid of humanoids. What, he asks, should I make of that? Now let us imagine that in mysterious ways he learns English, takes you up to his platform, shows you his data, and asks you to explain the rationale for the five-two regularity. Why not four-three, or six-one, and so on? Understanding, as he now does, our culture and that schools are educational institutions, it must be, he asserts, that there is an unassailable *educational* rationale for the five-two regularity. What is it? The answer, of course, is that historically the five-two regularity has less to do with an educational rationale and more to do with religion, changing features of work, child labor, and other factors. It is not a regularity derived from a clear logic, theory, or evidence.

Similarly, our visitor from outer space will have discerned another obvious regularity: every school day during the school year, every year from first grade to the end of high school, a "big" person does something with "little" people in regard to numbers. Why every day, month, year? Why forty minutes or so each day? Why not all day everyday for a month, two months, and so on? There are, our visitor tells us, a universe of alternatives. Why this particular regularity? And, again, he says that there must be some very good educational reasons why this one regularity was chosen, why other alternatives were considered, tried, and rejected—that is, why this regularity is considered the most conducive for achieving educational goals. Our answer would be other than compelling. We are victims of the Panglossian belief that what is is the best of all possible alternatives. What is has to be. That is what in essence the Spanish teacher was saying.

It is now the conventional wisdom that schools have to change. We are at a point where we are more willing than ever before to confront the annoyingly provocative queries of the man from Mars about alternatives. I fear that as people confront these queries, they sense that they are going in a direction that will be so radical in its consequences, so strewn with obstacles and turmoil, so necessarily uncertain in outcomes, that they retreat from confrontation. Paradoxically, that fear reflects optimism on my part. My pessimism is reflected in a second fear, realistically grounded, that although the reformers speak the language of change, they are still unable to consider the kinds of questions our visitor from outer space raised. Let us not gloss over the attitude implied by his questions: that alternatives are not of a piece, that their virtues (if any) do not reside in novelty but in their salience for achieving educational aims, that aims should inform means and not be transformed by them, that the more you narrow your universe of alternatives—worse yet, if you are not even aware that there is a universe of alternatives—the more you ensure that the existing regularities are in no danger of change.

I am not aware of any report by a commission appointed to recommend educational reform that characterizes its recommendations as radical or revolutionary. Those adjectives smack too much of political movements on the extreme left of the political continuum. If the aim of some of these reports is to bring about radical change, that aim is cloaked in language that obscures the intent. To say that, however, attributes aims to these reports that the report writers did not intend—that is, they seek no radical change, the system stays pretty much as it is, and what exists must be improved, not discarded. If *radical* implies getting at the root of a problem, these reports are the polar opposite of radical. I am by no means alone in this view. If anything characterizes the attitude toward these reports of people in diverse groups—those with an interest or stake in what happens in and to our schools—it is not renewed hope but a puzzled pessimism, puzzled because they want to be hopeful or optimistic and yet cannot understand why recommended changes should have the desired consequences. As one person said to me: "I view these reports the way I do an alcoholic's promise to go on the wagon. How many times can you be disappointed?" Actuarially speaking, this person was making a prediction that the future will confirm.

What is the message we want to convey to school people?

We challenge schools and communities to look at education in a whole new light. Our goal is to nurture innovative—even radical—new approaches, not reward entrenched conventional wisdom. We don't intend to spend our money frivolously, but neither do we intend to fall into the trap of betting only on sure things. This means we'll be funding controversial strategies and programs— ones that ruffle feathers and raise eyebrows, but get results. To some, this may sound like a big risk. We see things differently. To us, the biggest risk in education is not taking one. It can be an era of unbounded promise and opportunity for all Americans, but only if we take bold action to turn our schools around. As a nation, we have no higher priority than ensuring our children gain the knowledge, skills, and critical thinking ability essential to their survival in a world of dizzying technological, economic, and social change. But America's schools are failing our young people and jeopardizing our nation's future. At stake is our nation's ability to compete with the economic powerhouse of Western Europe and Asia—and with it, the quality of life for generations of Americans to come.

Fine tuning, tinkering at the margins, doing what we are currently doing only better—these timid strategies aren't a formula for positive change. They're a formula for certain disaster. The hard reality is that radical change is long overdue in our public schools. Conquering persistent problems like tragically high dropout rates, lagging math and science performance, and abysmal reading and writing skills demands bold and innovative strategies. It's clear that traditional approaches aren't working, and that we must create fundamentally new learning environments that are more responsive to today's children.

We recognize that risk taking is often a lonely venture. All of us like to talk about new ideas and innovative strategies; none of us likes to fail. But risking failure is a necessary condition of charting new courses and it simply must be done. Fortunately, there are teachers and principals across America who are succeeding against all odds in making schools work. We want to find them and give them the money they need to get started and keep going.

We believe business can play an important role in improving our schools: namely, to encourage and fund risk taking and entrepreneurial change. To this end, we established the Next Century Schools Program. Next Century Schools is a $30 million challenge grant program established for elementary, middle, and secondary schools to undertake bold reforms to improve individual schools based on their individual needs.

Consistent with Next Century School's goal of stimulating radical but sustainable innovation in elementary and secondary education, the highest priority will be given to proposals incorporating two important elements:

1.  A shared commitment by the school and the community to make the program work, and a commitment for matching funds. This shared commitment can come from a combination of interested parties such as parents, teachers, the business community, and the social district.
2.  A plan for sustained, wide-ranging change that can be replicated throughout the district, state, or nation. Applicants must describe how they intend to continue and expand programs if they succeed, and how they foresee their program being used as a model for other schools.

Those are not my words but they reflect well an attitude with which I agree but which is not conveyed in the usual report. Radical, risk-taking, fruitless tinkering, controversial, failure as a way of learning—these words and phrases are not contained in the scores of reports on educational reform. The statement above does not contain proposals for reform; it does elaborate on an attitude without which proposals for and implementation of reforms will accomplish nothing. It is a statement by Louis V. Gerstner, Jr., of R.J.R. Nabisco, accompanying the announcement of his company's $30 million challenge grant program for elementary, middle, and high schools. It is called the Next Century Schools Program. Gerstner has put his money where his mouth is. He is no educator and he is not foisting his ideas on anyone. Like me, Gerstner recognizes that what has been done to improve schools has not worked. He avoids criticism and scapegoating. He has put his finger on several crucial problems: how to foster radical reexamination of the axioms and traditions undergirding our thinking, how to provide incentives for such a reexamination, and how to get people to understand that risk taking should not be viewed as frivolous and that failure can have productive consequences. Gerstner wants our children to be better critical thinkers. In essence, he is saying to educators and the general public: heal thyself. If critical thinking is not a notable feature of educational reformers, why should we expect it in students? If Gerstner is no educator, his challenge is the most seminal one that has been put to educators *and* the general public.

In this final chapter I have advocated for a particular overarching aim for students. I am quite aware that students who enter our schools vary dramatically on such variables as race, ethnicity, family structure and background, economic status, housing, neighborhood, language skills, and religious affiliation. It is a daunting heterogeneity that complicates the task of the educators to a degree that most people underestimate. Nothing I have said in this book should be interpreted as suggesting that if my diagnoses are accepted and actions consistent with them are undertaken, all will be well. As I said earlier, we are not dealing with problems that have scientific solutions in the sense that four divided by two has a solution or that the polio vaccine is a solution. We are not dealing with problems that, once solved, do not have to be solved again and again. The American Constitution was not a solution. It was a blueprint of values, aims, and institutional arrangements that the writers knew would require interpretation, reinterpretation, and change. That provision was made for an amendment process was not fortuitous. The writers were too wise, too knowledgeable about human societies and institutions, to believe that the Constitution provided solutions to problems of the past, present, and future. It is to their everlasting credit that they were clear about what they believed people are, wanted, and deserved—the overarching values and aims that should inform governmental actions. They needed no lessons about the inevitable imperfections of society and its people. The Constitution is not comprehensible apart from the writers' agreement (which was not total) about what people are, want, and deserve. In advocating for the overarching aim I have discussed in this chapter, I have tried to make clear what I believe the children who come to our schools are, want, and deserve. Our task is to take that seriously, and in doing so, to be as bold, courageous, radical, and revolutionary as the Founding Fathers. They knew that the Articles of Confederation were inadequate and potentially lethal to the growth and security of a fledgling society. As long as they allowed themselves to stay within the confines of these articles, the major problems would be intractable to remedy. Confronting that intractability, they entered history.

## Note

1. It is more complicated than that because unless the teacher begins with an understanding of her or his particular way of learning, *a* way among several "learning styles" each of which is characteristic of some but not all people, each of which is legitimate in that it is productive for some learners, the teacher will be unable to grasp the different starting points of students, that is, flex to their individual styles. No one more than David Hunt of the Ontario Institute for

Studies in Education has stated this problem so clearly, re-searched it so thoroughly, and applied it so productively to real teachers and real classrooms. His book (1987) has the very apt title, *Beginning with Ourselves. In Practice, Theory, and Human Affairs.* As best as I can determine, his work and book have had no influence in teacher-training programs.

# References

Blatt, B. *Christmas in Purgatory.* Boston: Allyn & Bacon, 1970a.

Blatt, B. *Exodus from Pandemonium.* Boston: Allyn & Bacon, 1970b.

Buxton, C. *Adolescents in Schools.* New Haven: Yale University Press, 1973.

Cowen, E. L., and others. "State-Level Dissemination of a Program for Early Detection and Prevention of School Maladjustment." *Professional Psychology: Research and Practice,* 1989, *20* (5), 309–314.

Farber, B. "Stress and Burn-out in the American Teacher: Two Decades of Blaming the Helper" (tentative title). San Francisco: Jossey-Bass, forthcoming.

Frost, C. F., Wakeley, J. H., and Ruh, R. A. *The Scanlon Plan for Organizational Development: Identity, Participation, and Equity.* East Lansing: Michigan State University, 1974.

Goodlad, J. *A Place Called School.* New York: McGraw-Hill, 1984.

Hawley, W. D. "Missing Pieces of the Educational Reform Agenda: Or, Why the First and Second Waves May Miss the Boat." *Educational Administration Quarterly,* November 1988, pp. 416–437.

Hawley, W. D. "Looking Backward at Education Reform." *Education Week*, November 1, 1989, p. 32.

Hunt, D. E. *Beginning with Ourselves. In Practice, Theory, and Human Affairs.* Cambridge, Mass.: Brookline Books, 1987.

Johnson, D., and Johnson, R. *Learning Together and Alone.* Englewood Cliffs, N.J.: Princeton-Hall, 1987.

Johnson, D., Johnson, R., and Maruyama, G. "Interdependence and Interpersonal Attraction Among Heterogeneous and Homogeneous Individuals: A Theoretical Formulation and a Meta-Analysis of the Research." *Review of Educational Research*, 1983, *68*, 446–452.

Kammeraad-Campbell, S. *Doc. The Story of Dennis Littky and His Fight for a Better School.* Chicago: Contemporary Books, 1989.

Mehan, H. "Microcomputers in Classrooms: Educational Technology or Social Practice?" *Anthropology and Education Quarterly*, 1989, *20*, 4–21.

Rossiter, C. *1787: The Grand Convention.* New York: New American Library, 1966.

Sarason, S. B. *The Creation of Settings and the Future Societies.* San Francisco: Jossey-Bass, 1972; Cambridge, Mass.: Brookline Books, 1989 (paperback).

Sarason, S. B. *The Culture of the School and the Problem of Change.* (2ⁿᵈ ed.) Boston: Allyn & Bacon, 1982.

Sarason, S. B. *Schooling in America: Scapegoat and Salvation.* New York: Free Press, 1983.

Sarason, S. B. *Caring and Compassion in Clinical Practice: Issues in the Selection, Training, and Behavior of Helping Professionals.* San Francisco: Jossey-Bass, 1985.

Sarason, S. B., Davidson, K., and Blatt, B. *The Preparation of Teachers: An Unstudied Problem in Education.* Cambridge, Mass: Brookline Books, 1988.

Sarason, S. B. *The Challenge of Art to Psychology.* New Haven: Yale University Press, 1990.

Sarason, S. B., and others, *Psychology in Community Settings.* New York: Wiley, 1966.

Sharan, S. "Cooperative Learning in Small Groups: Recent Methods and Effects of Achievement, Attitudes, and Ethnic Relations." *Review of Educational Research*, 1980. *50*, 241–271.

Sharan, S., and Sharan, Y. "Changing Instructional Methods and the Culture of the School." In N. Wyner (ed.), *Current Perspectives on School Culture*. Cambridge, Mass.: Brookline Books, forthcoming.

Sharan, S., and others. *Cooperative Learning in the Classroom: Research in Segregated Schools*. Hillsdale, N.J.: Erlbaum and Associates, 1984.

Singer, J. "Persuasion." *Michigan Law Review*, 1989, *87*, 2442–2458.

Slavin, R. *Cooperative Learning*. New York: Longman, 1983.

Slavin, R., and others (eds.). *Learning to Cooperate, Cooperating to Learn*. New York: Plenum, 1985.

Timar, T. "The Politics of School Restructuring." *Phi Delta Kappan*, 1989, *71* (4), 264–275.

Whitehead, A. N. *The Aims of Education*. New York: Mentor Books, 1929.

# INDEX